Three In One
Dot to Dot, Puzzle and Coloring Geometric Patterns Book

This book belongs to

. . . .

Author: Mohamad Aljanabi , © 2020 Mohamad Aljanabi Rights

Instructions

1. Step one: using hp pencil draw a line between the dots as illusteated below.

   You can start from any dot you wish.

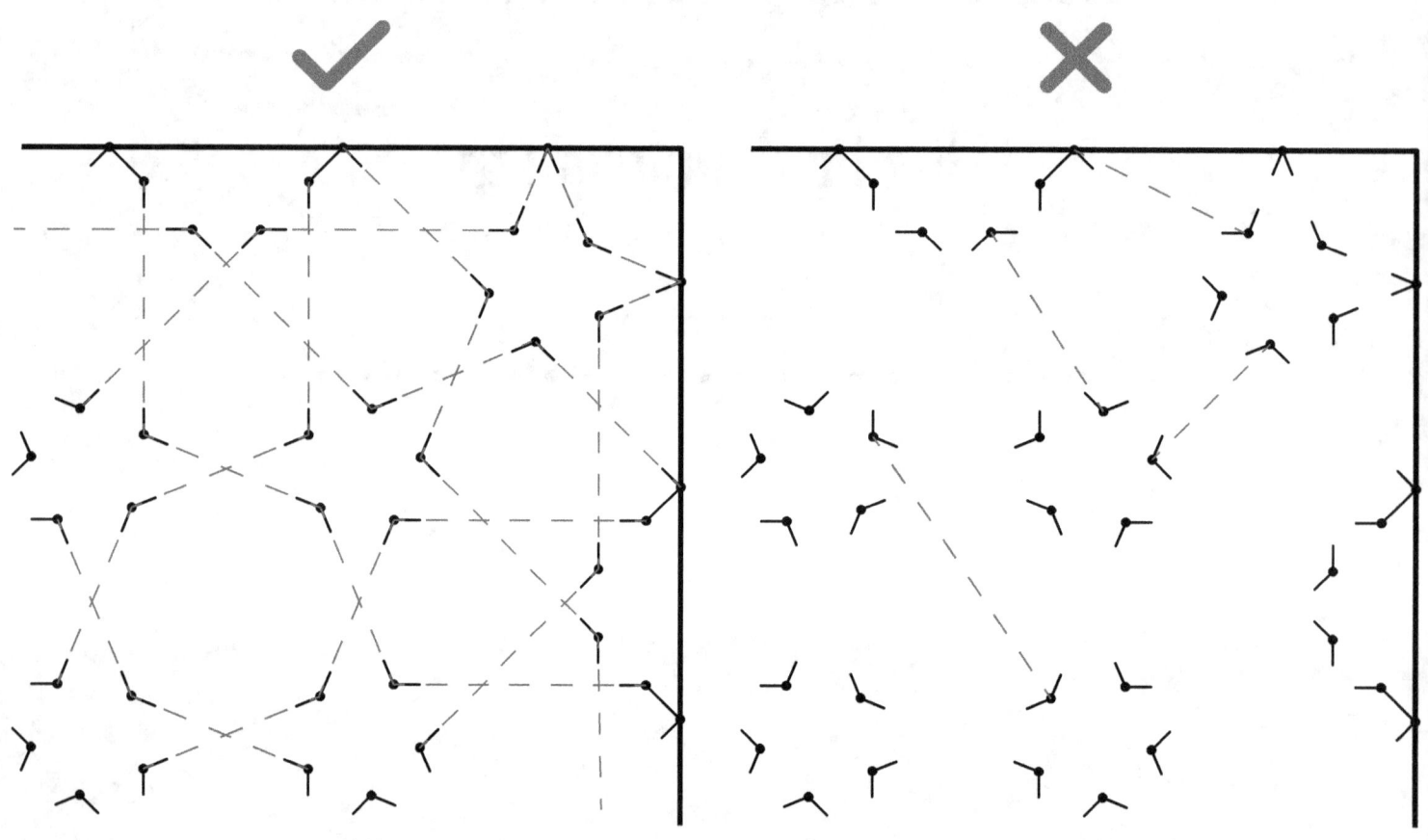

2. Step two: Step two: choose contrasting colors to color the shapes.

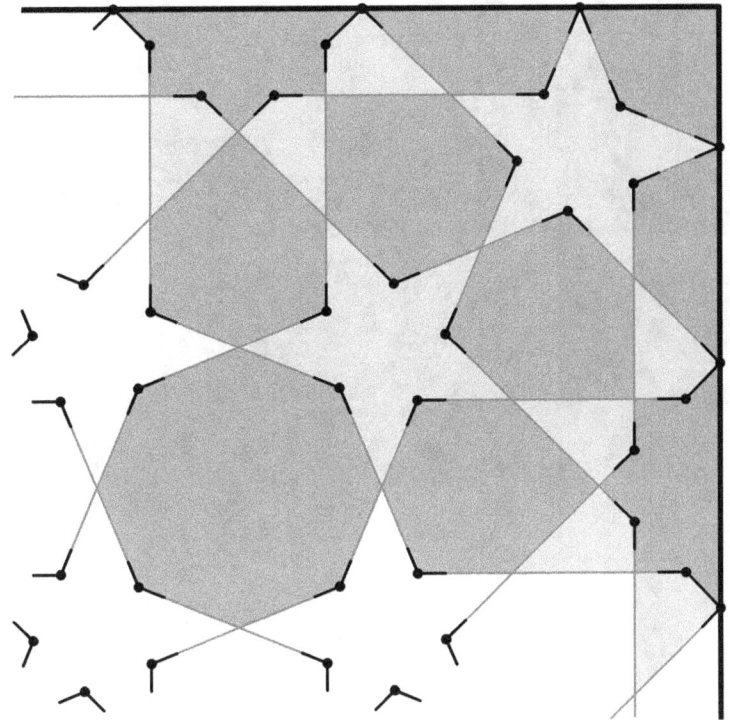

3. Step three: go over the lines between the shapes with a 0.5 mm or larger marker

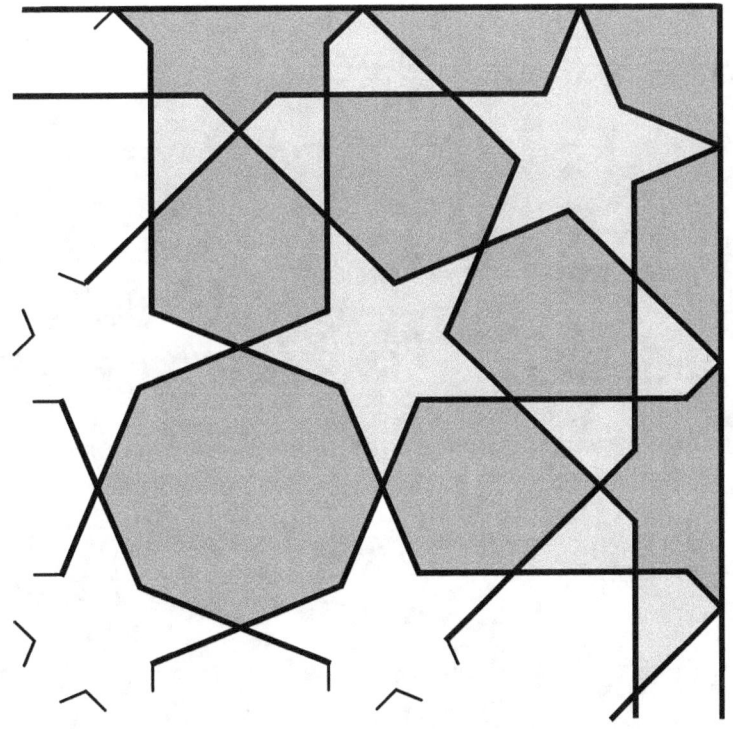

Solution on page: 66

5

Solution on page: 67

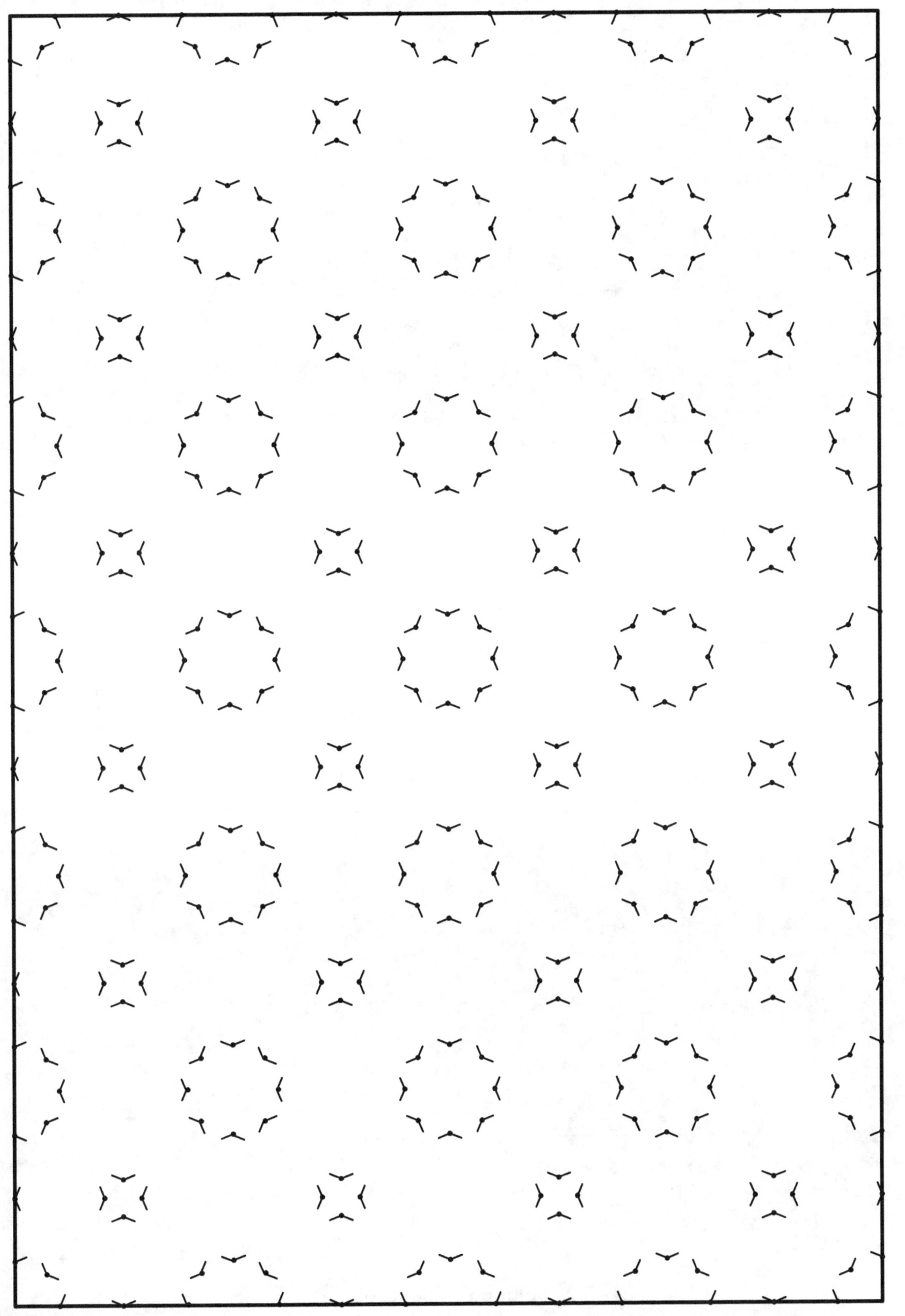

Solution on page: 68

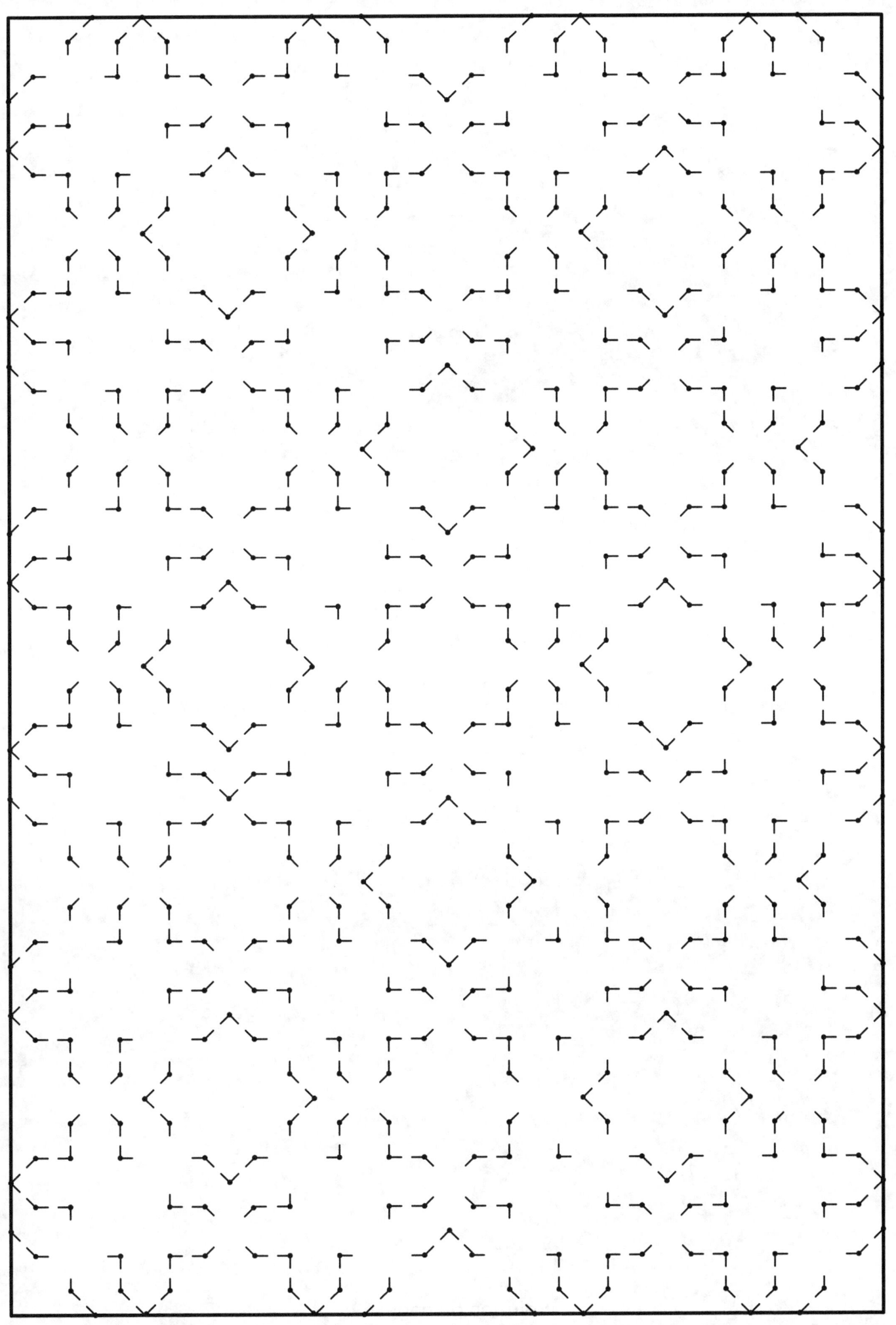

Solution on page: 69

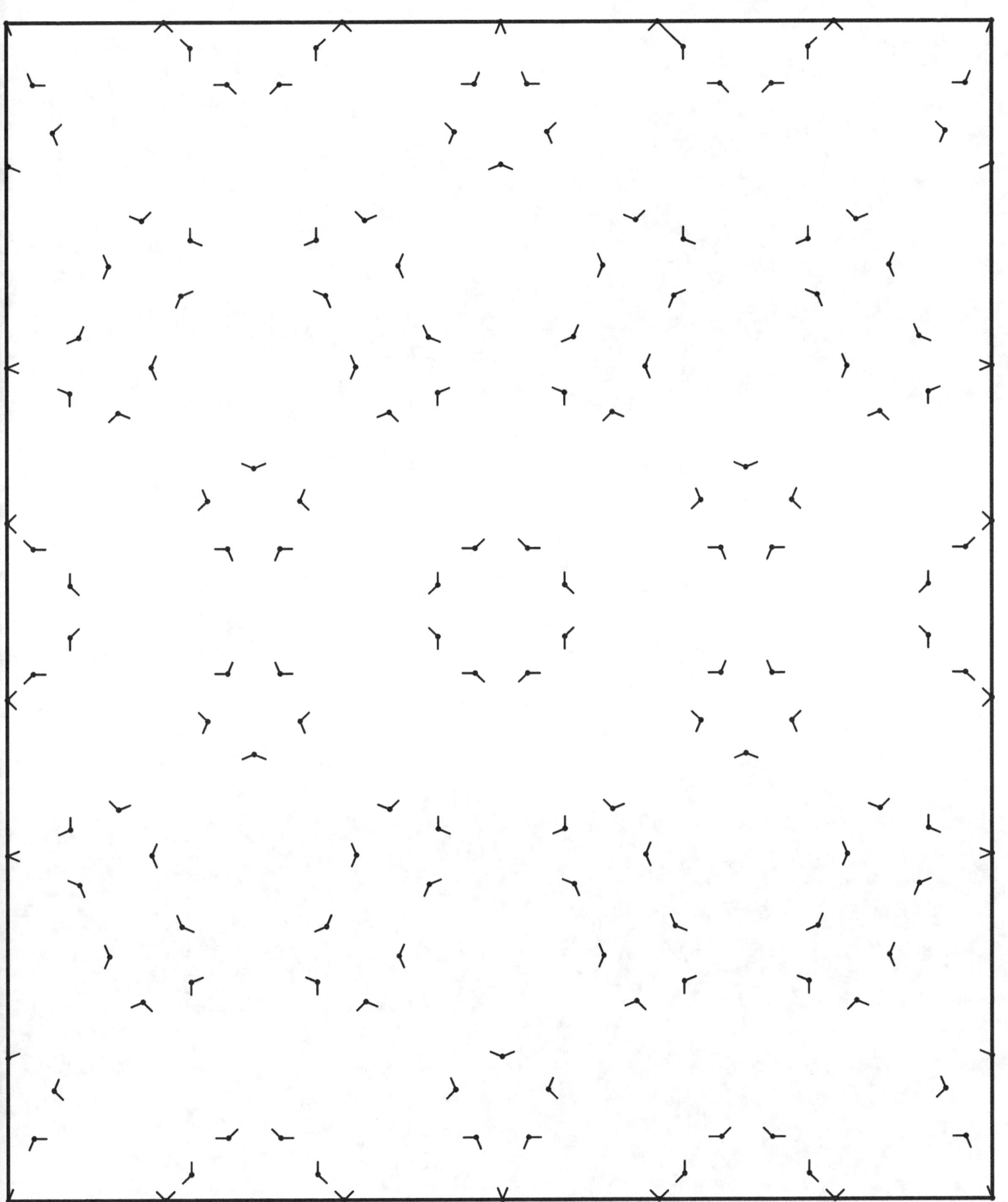

Solution on page: 70

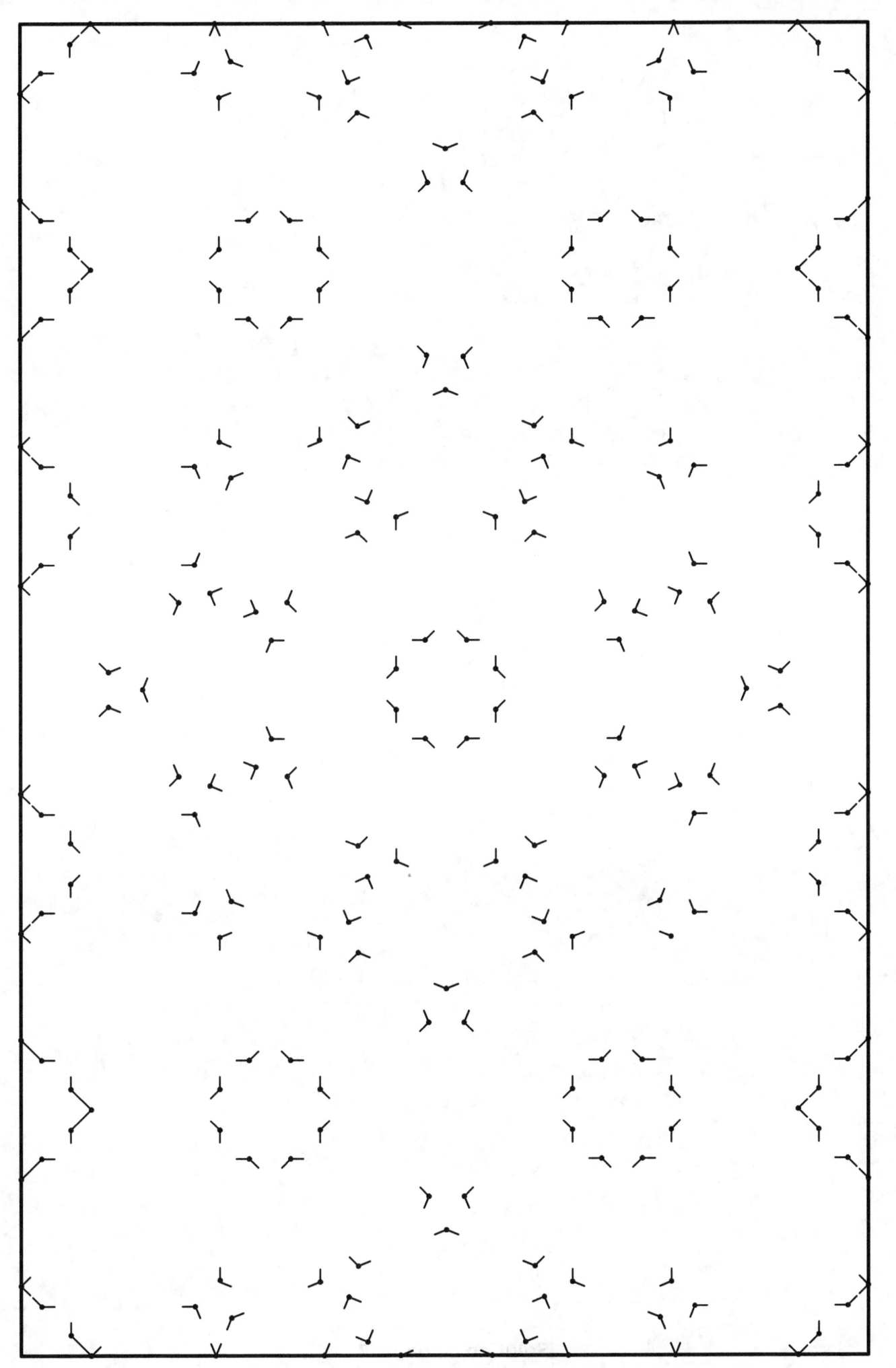

Solution on page: 71

Solution on page: 72

Solution on page: 73

19

Solution on page: 74

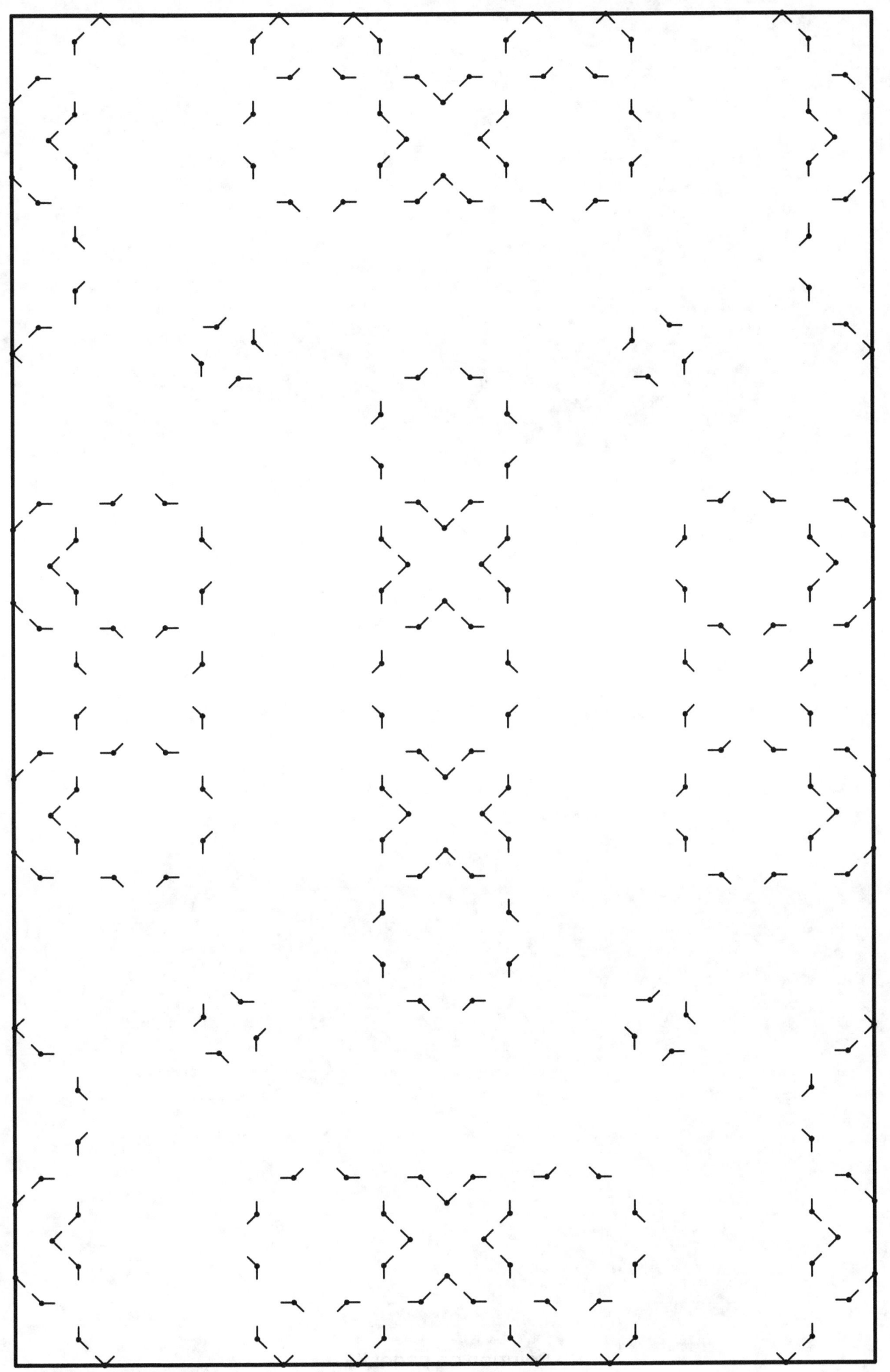

Solution on page: 75

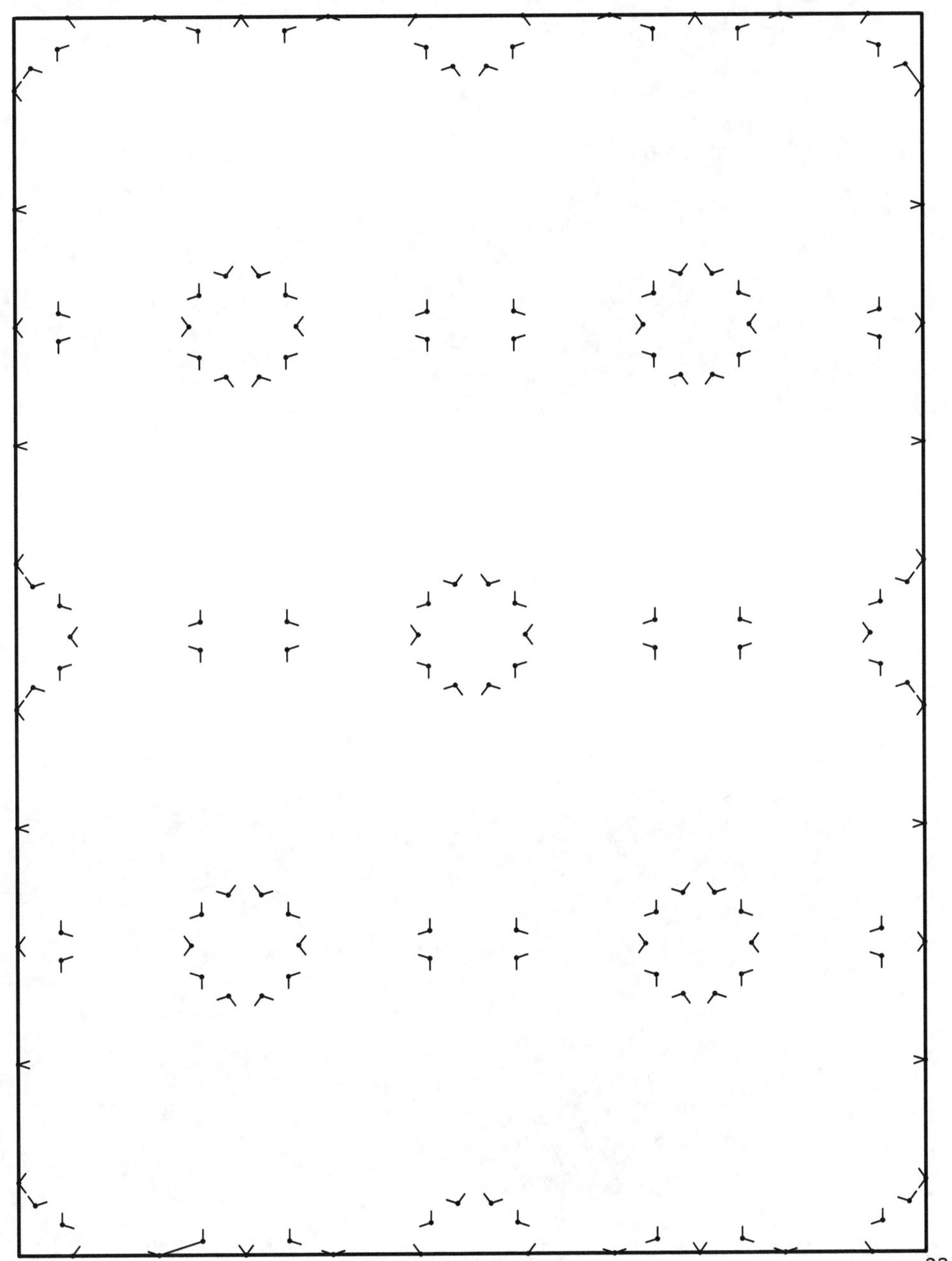

Solution on page: 76

25

Solution on page: 77

Solution on page: 78

29

Solution on page: 79

Solution on page: 80

Solution on page: 81

Solution on page: 82

37

Solution on page: 83

39

Solution on page: 84

Solution on page: 85

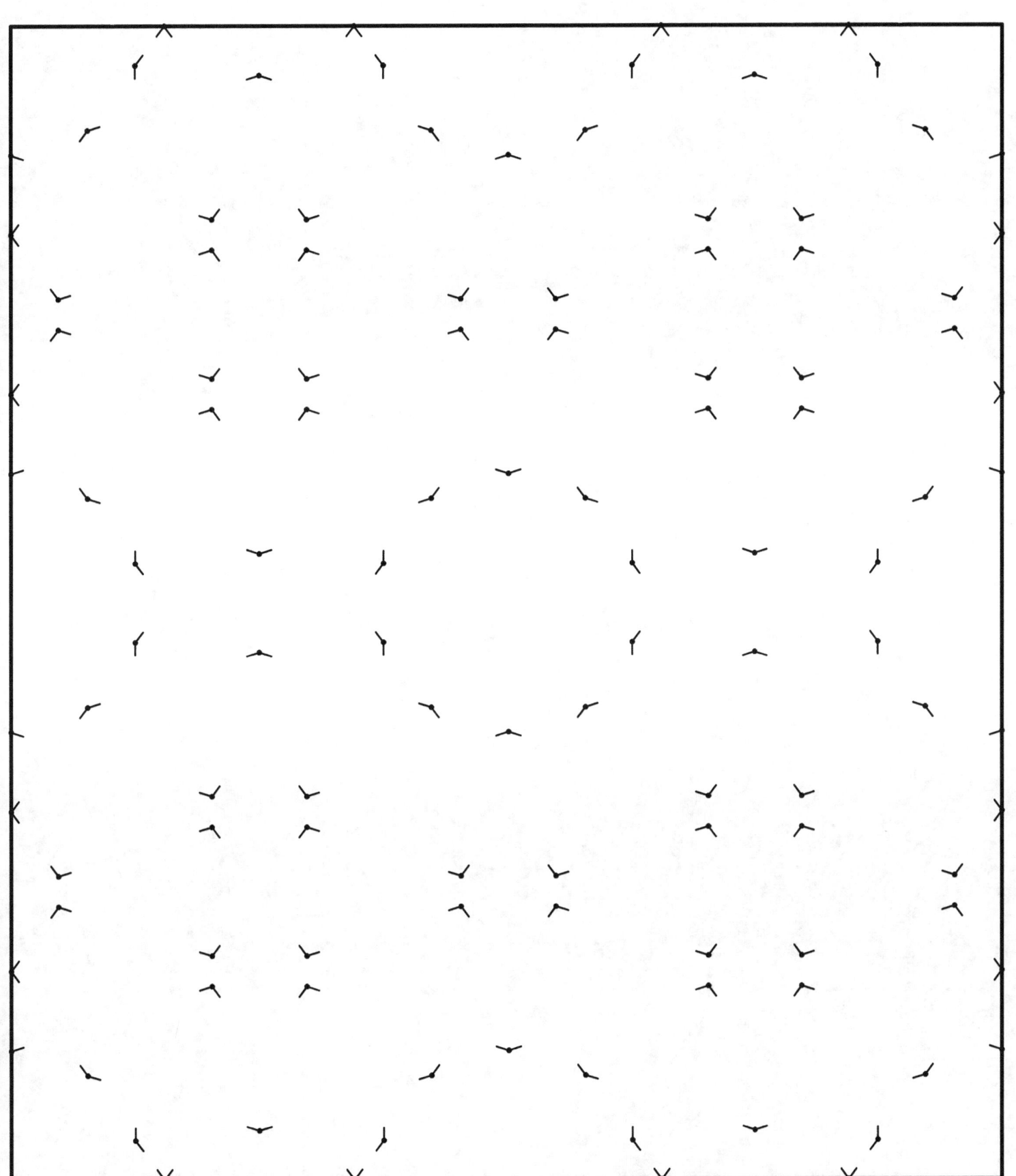

Solution on page: 86

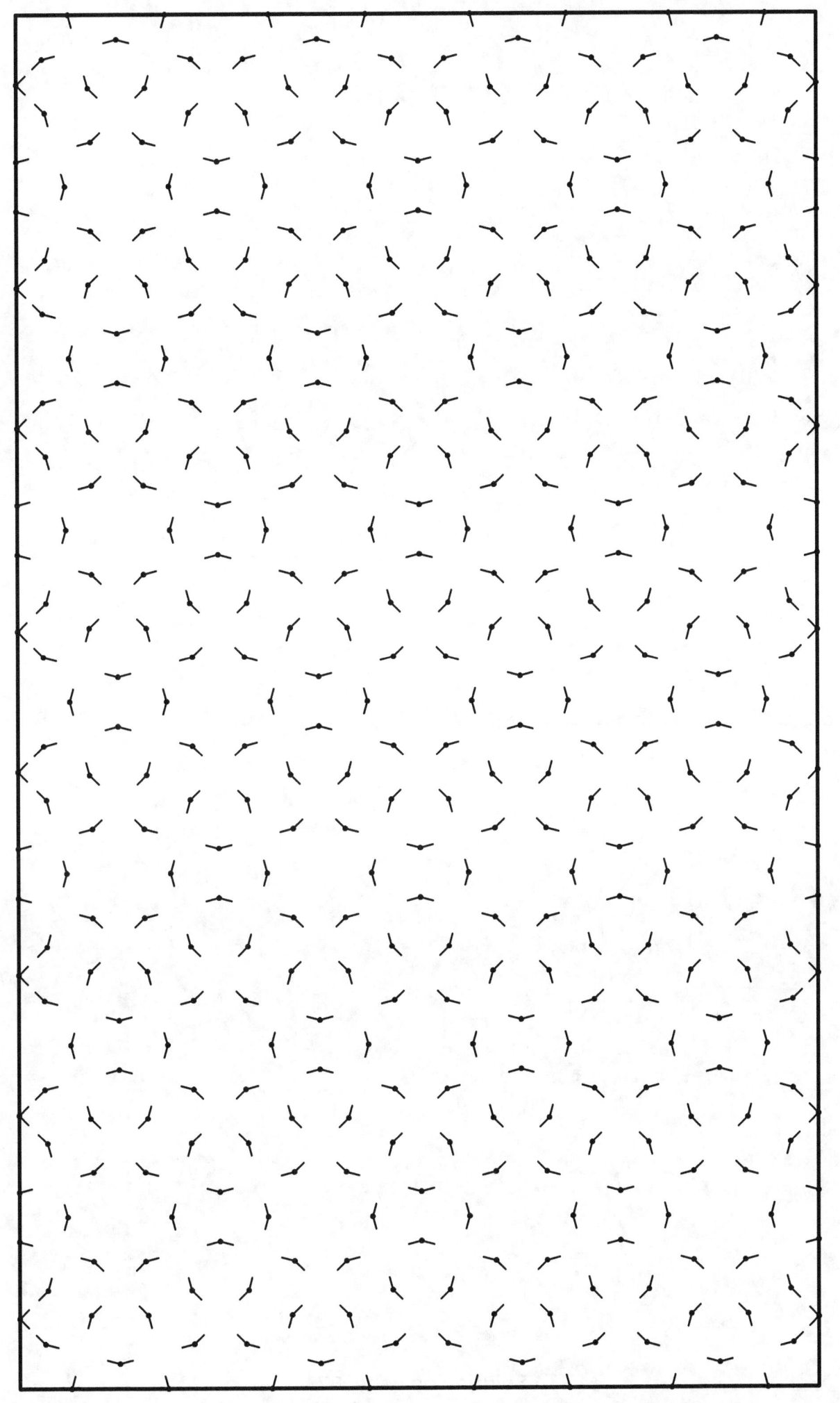

Solution on page: 88

Solution on page: 89

51

Solution on page: 90

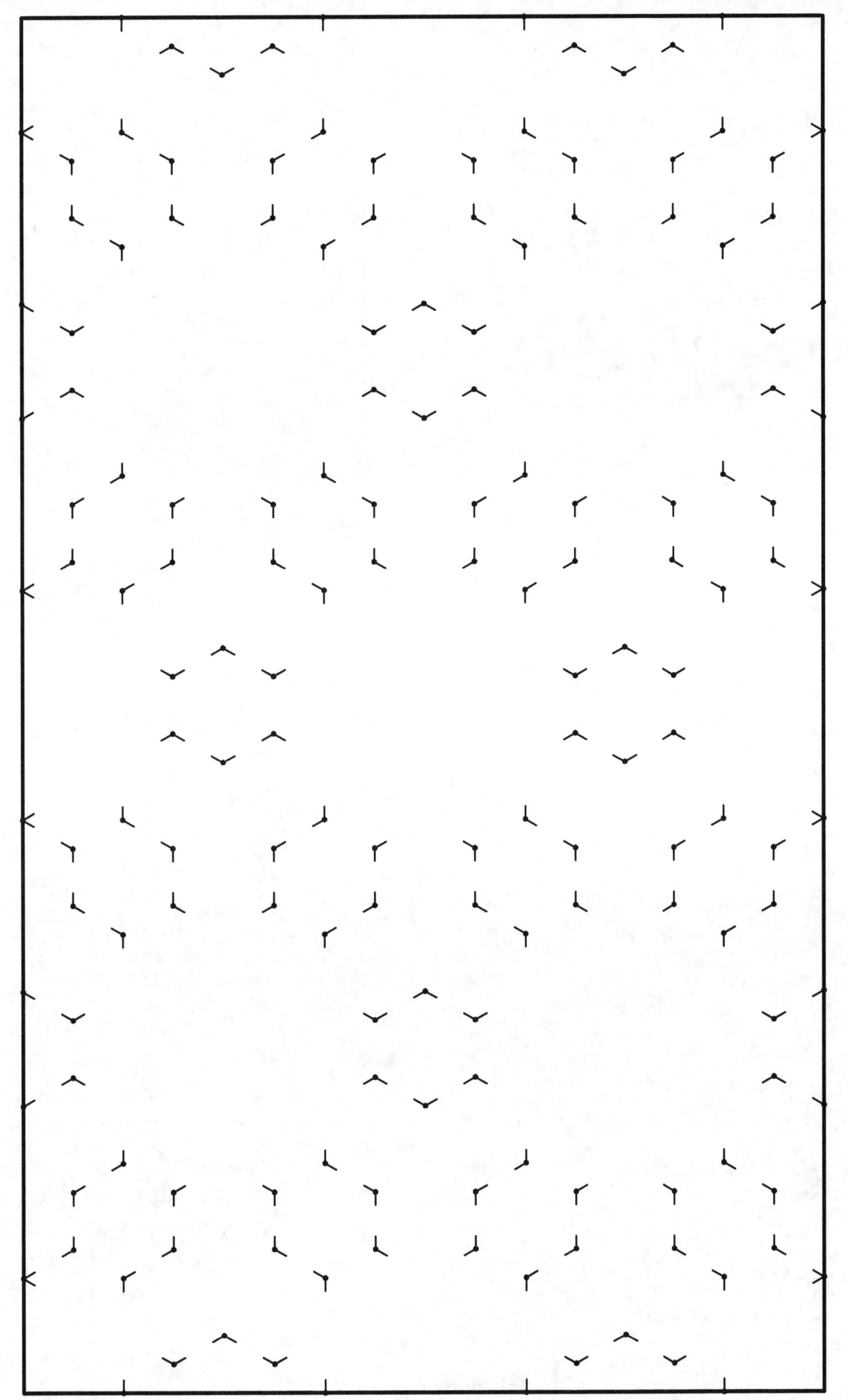

Solution on page: 91

Solution on page: 92

57

Solution on page: 93

Solution on page: 94

61

Solution on page: 95

63

Soulution for the puzzels

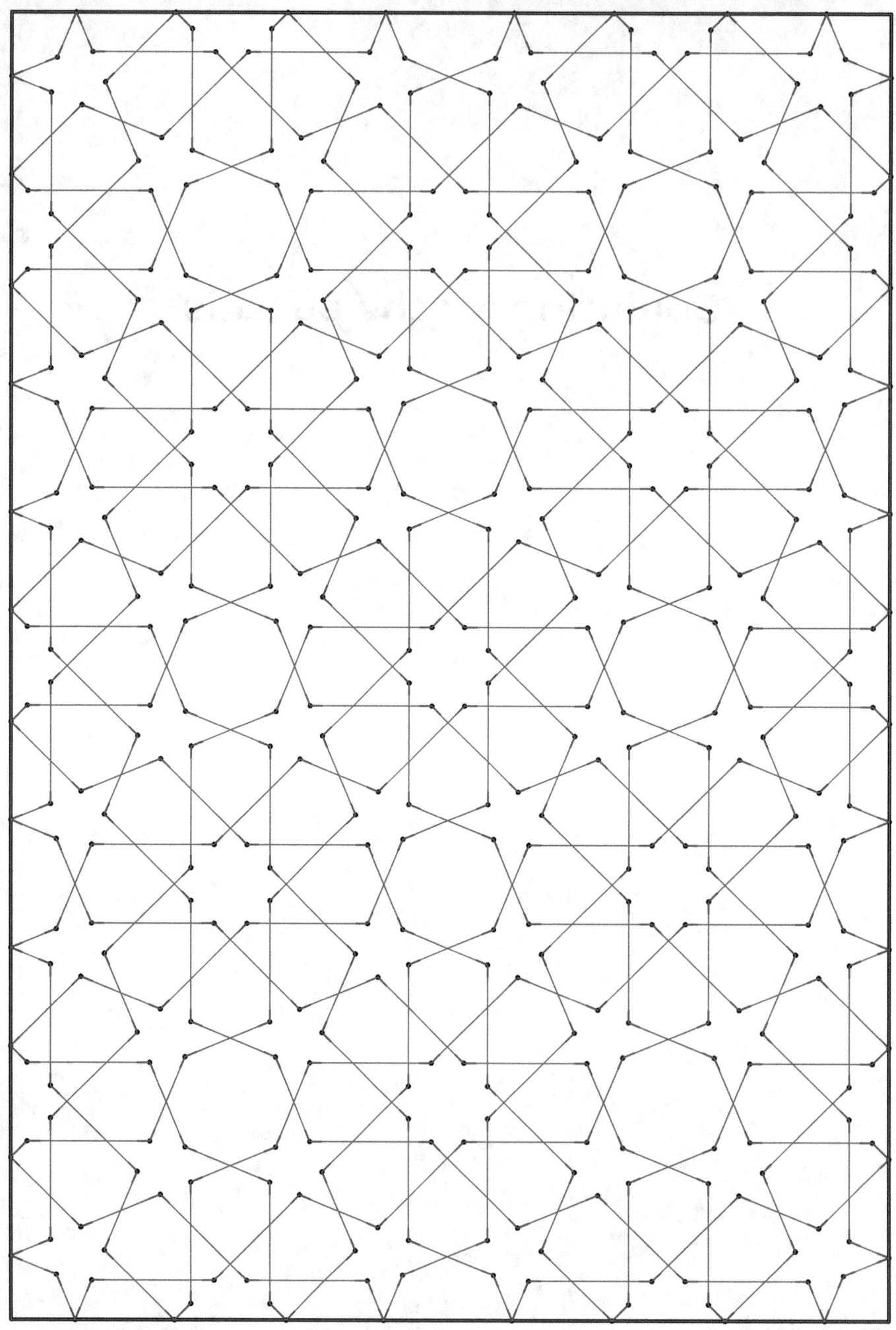

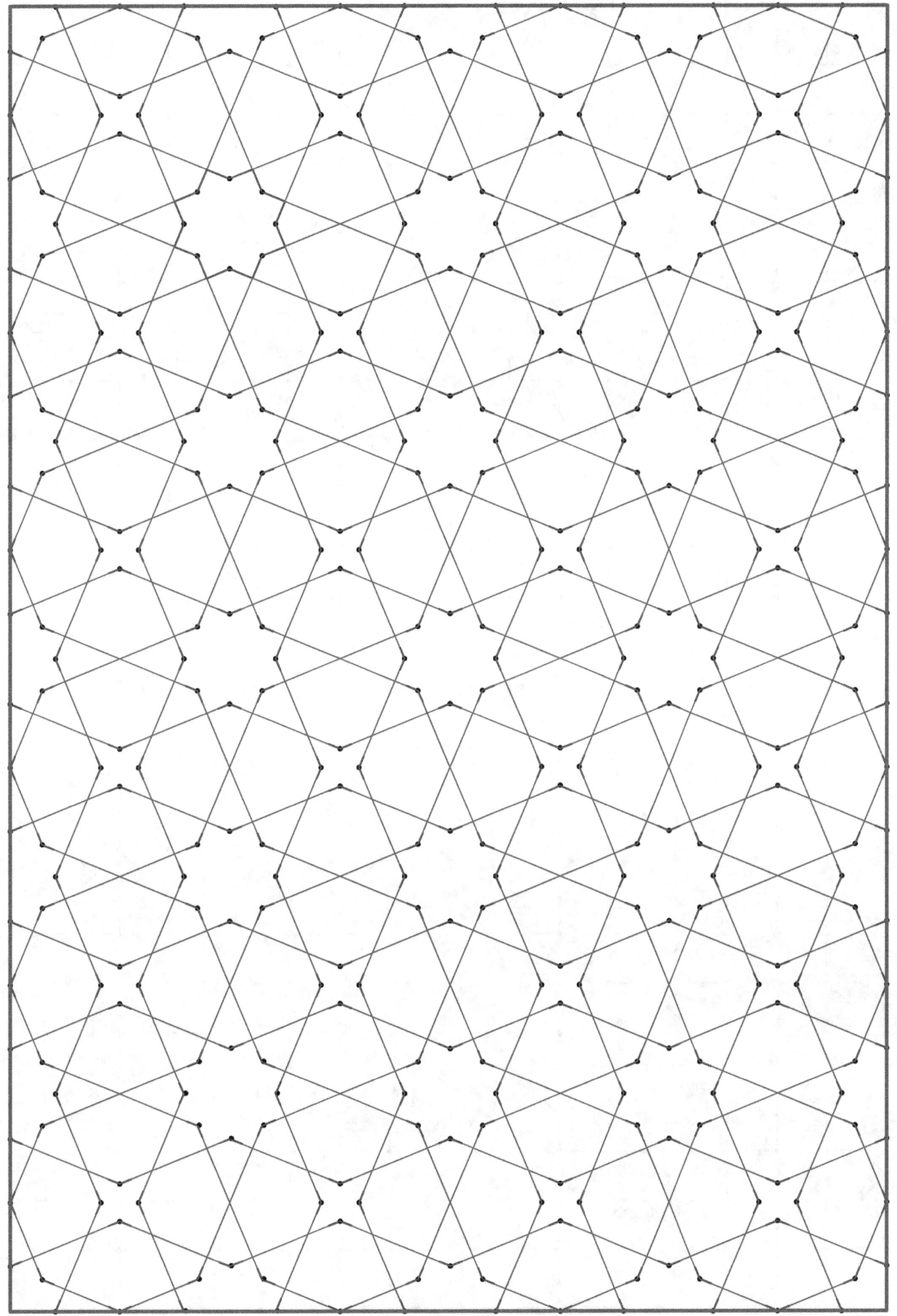

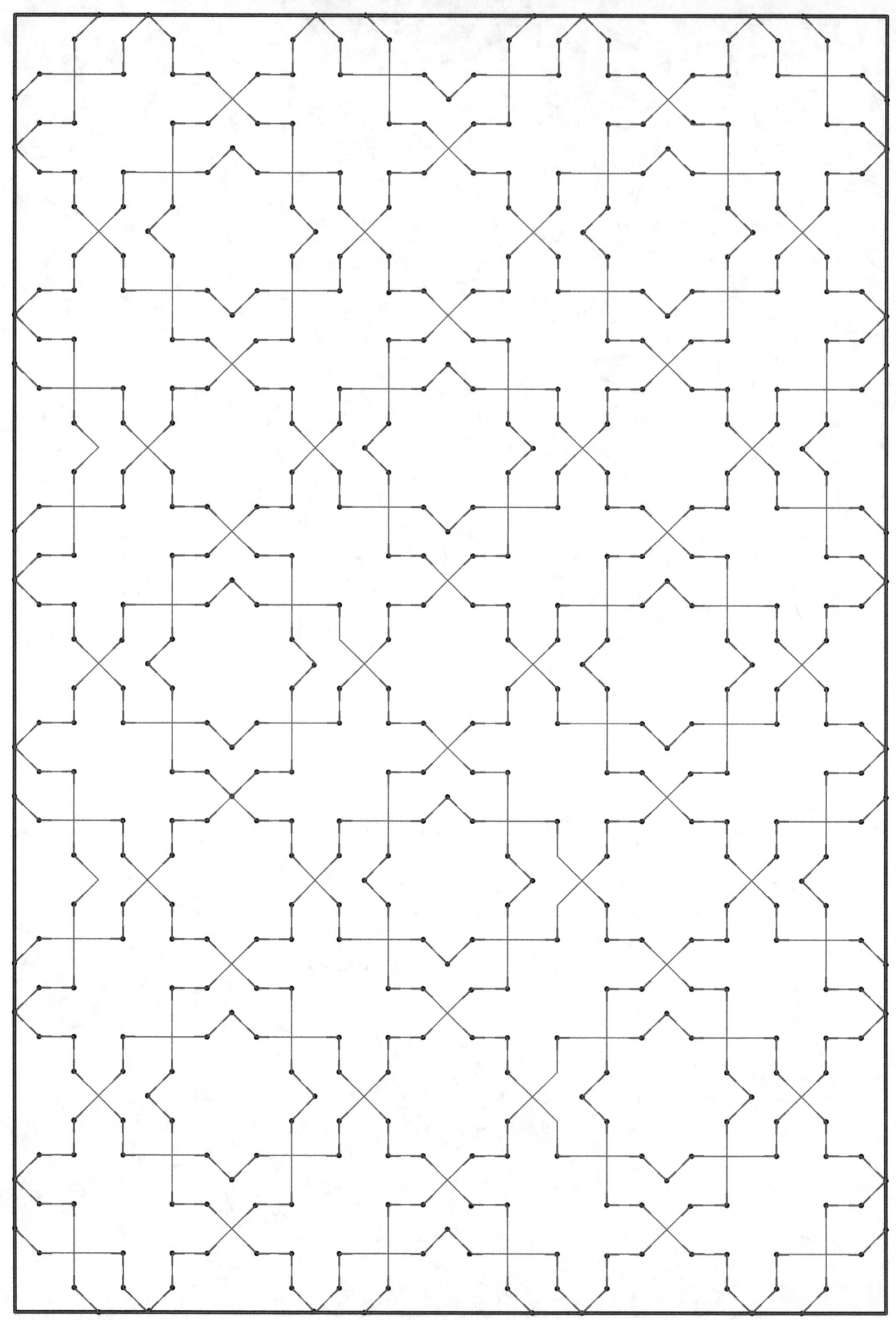

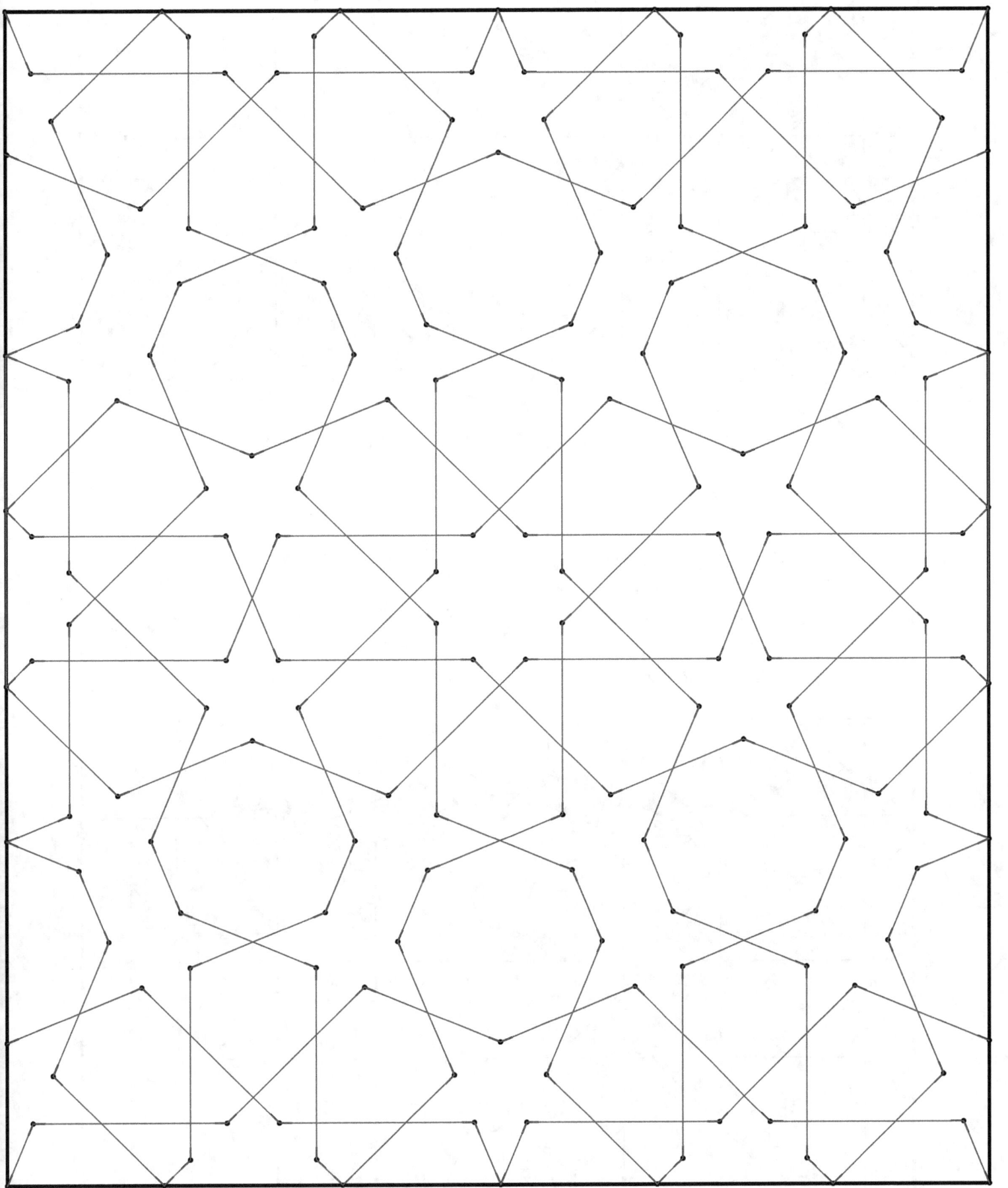

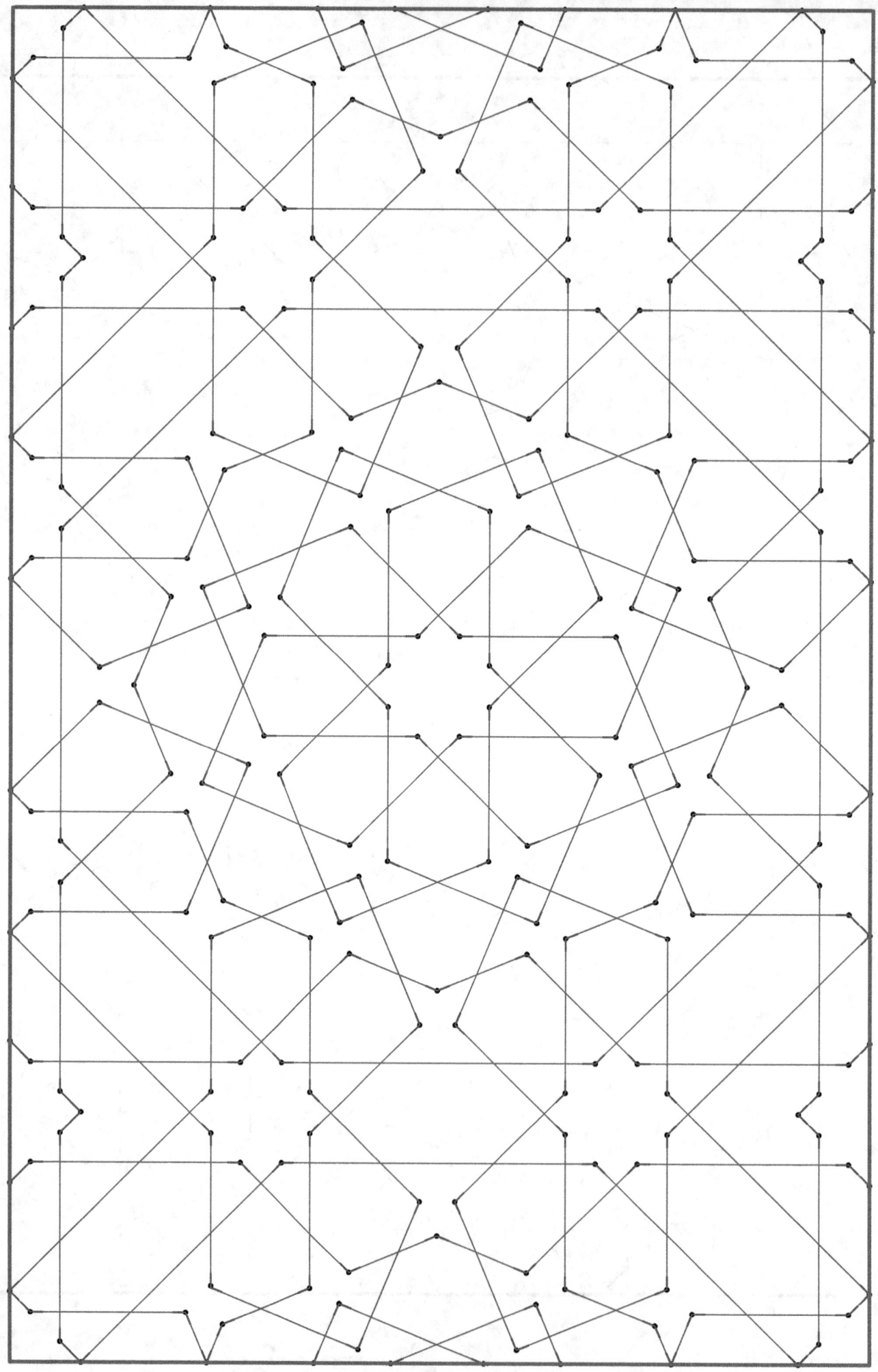

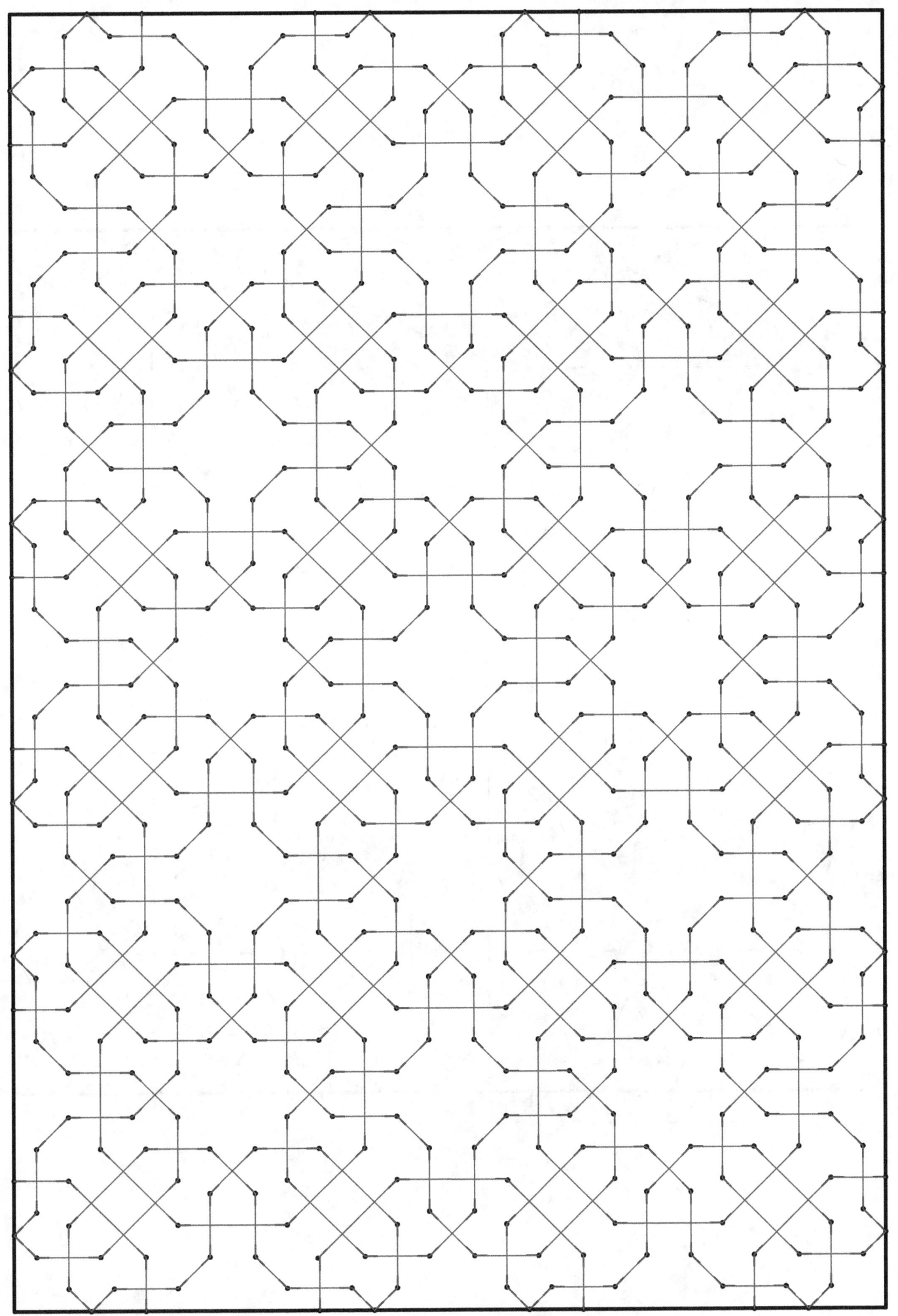

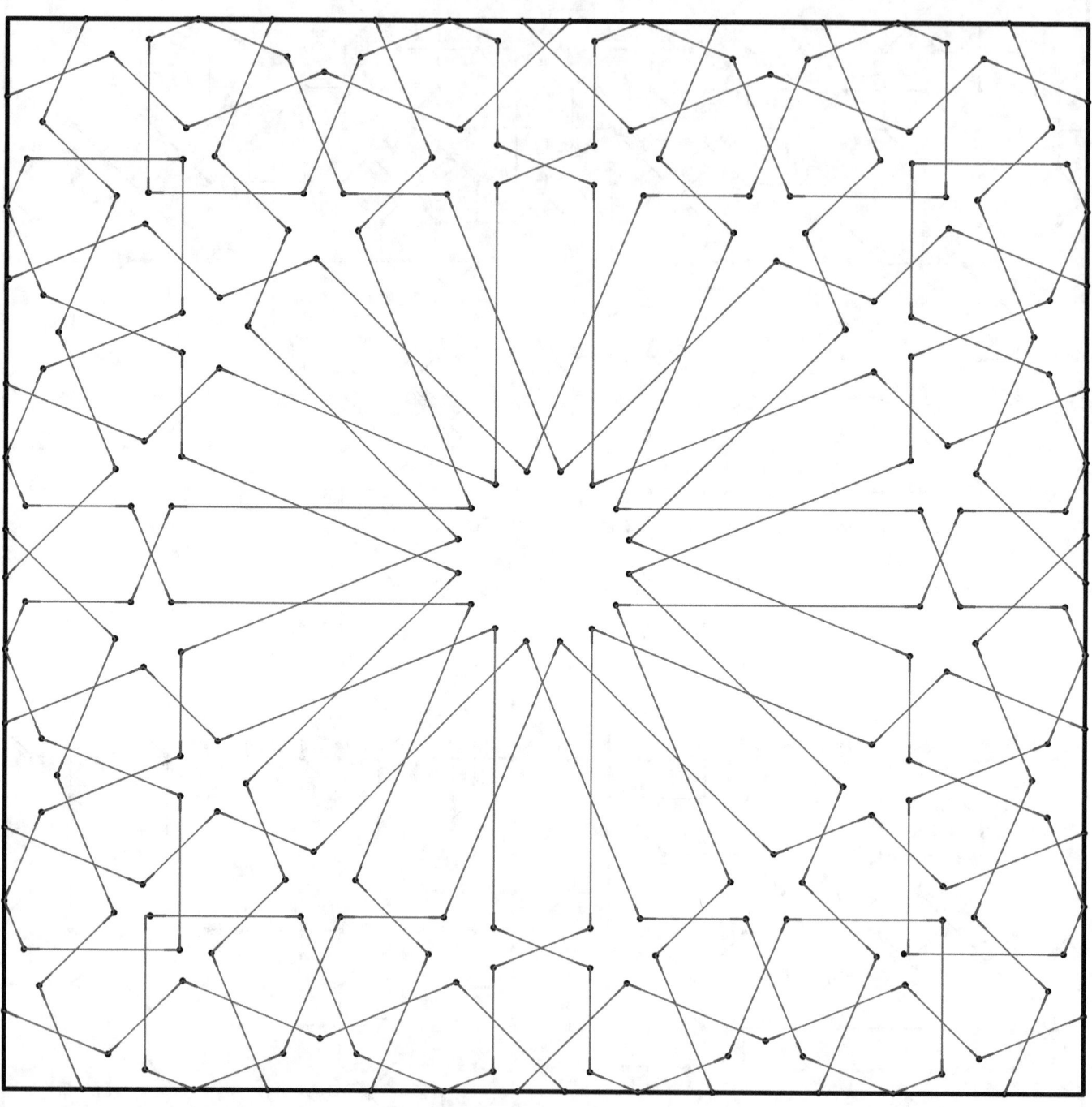

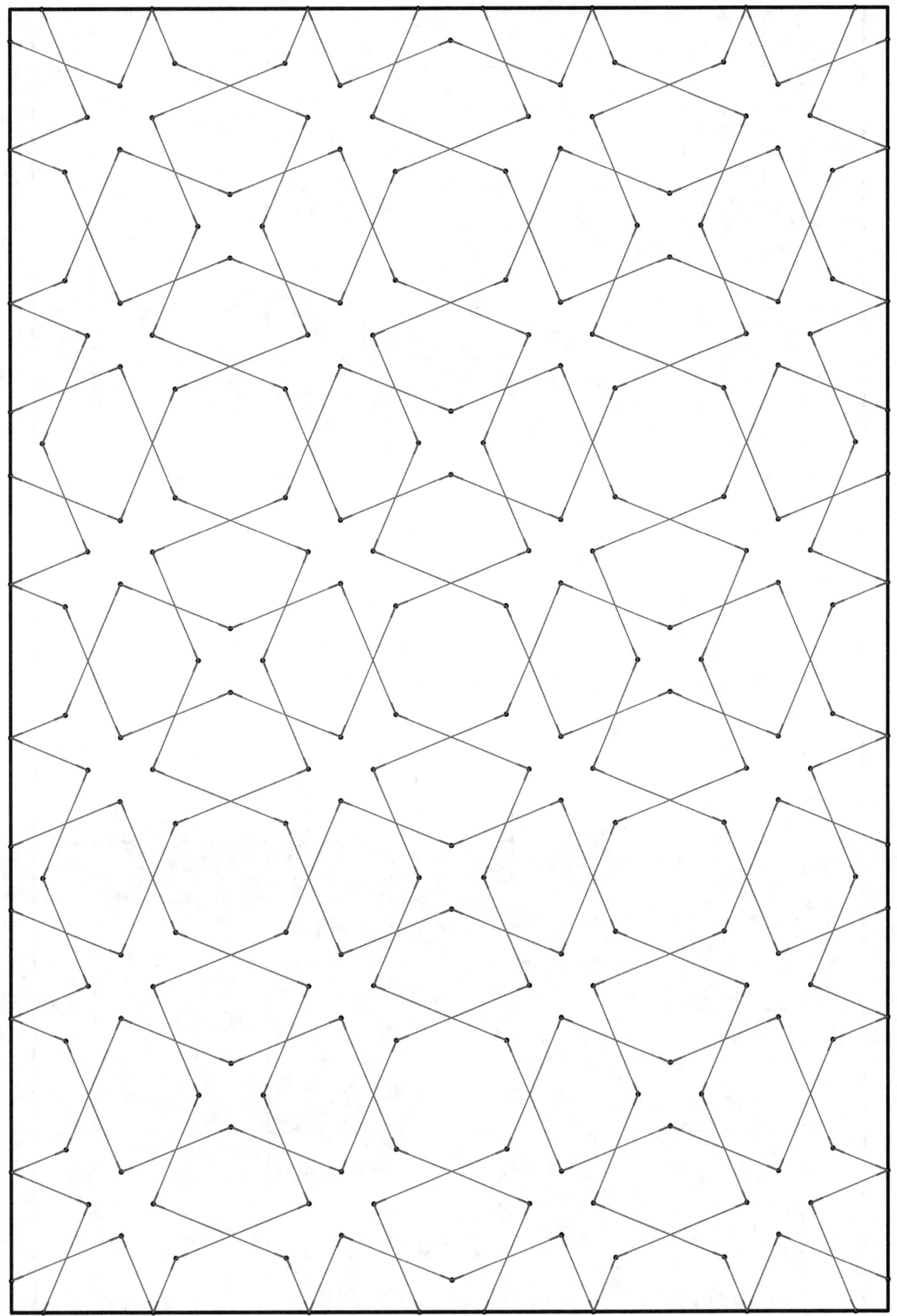

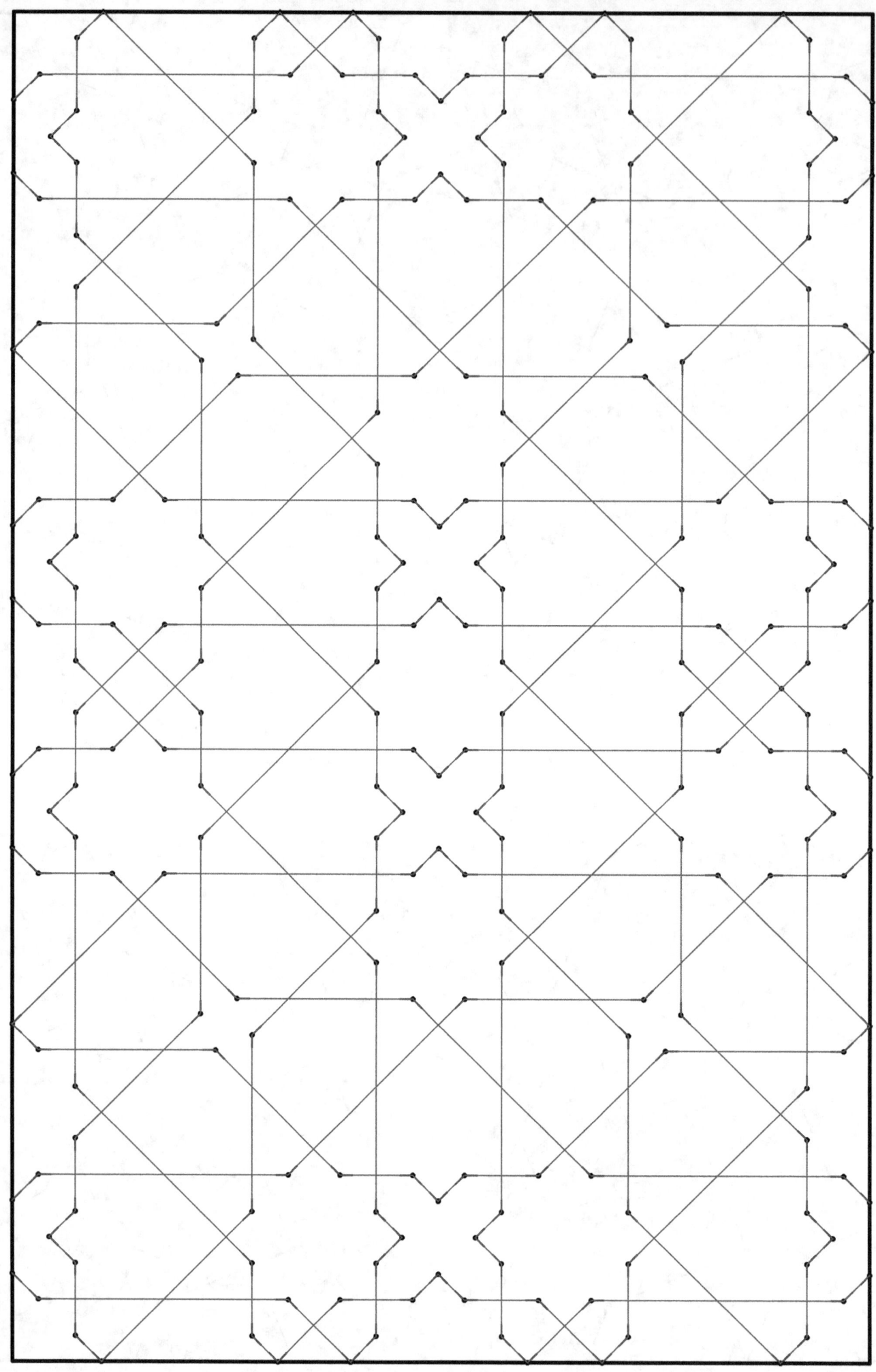

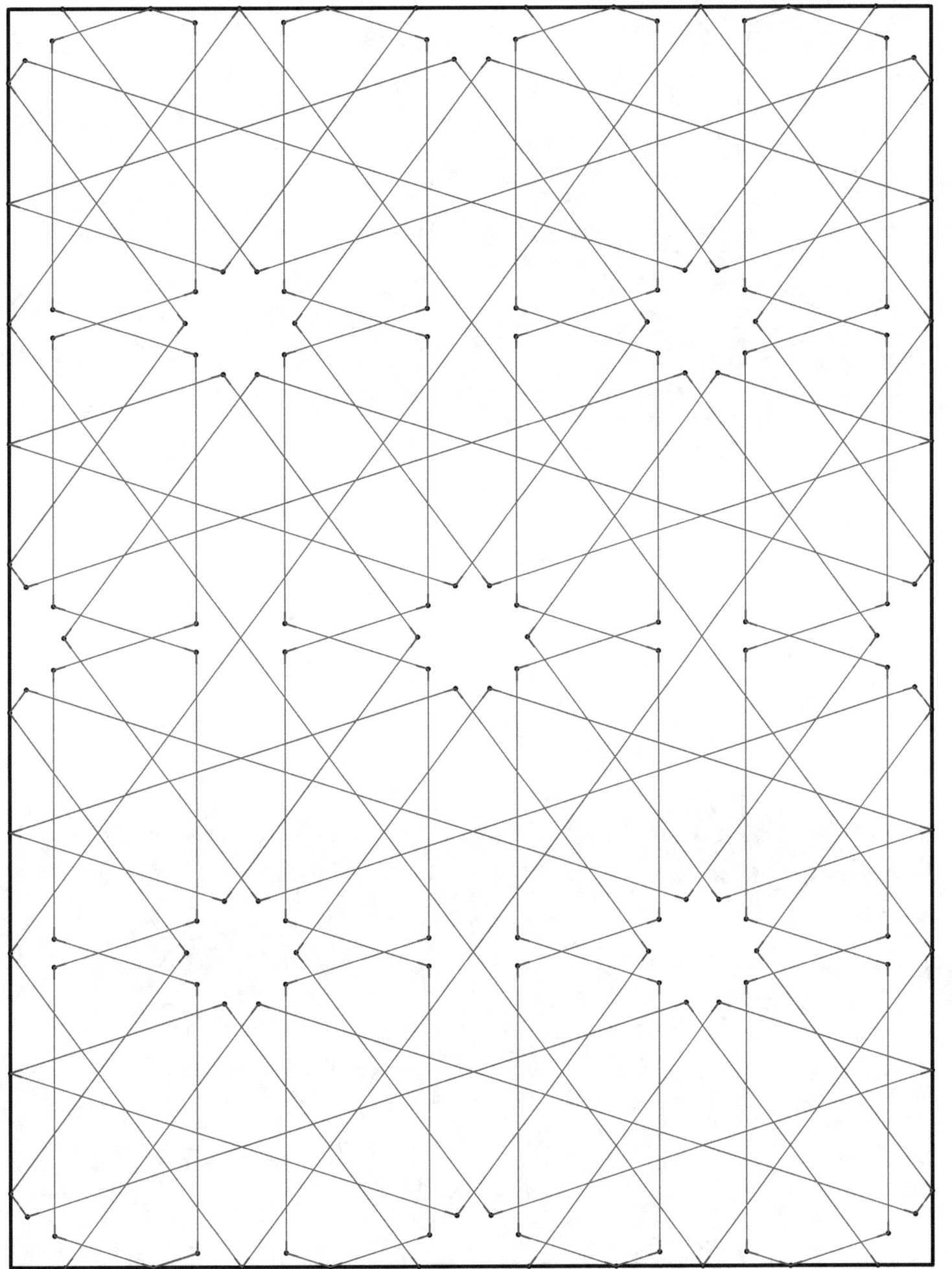

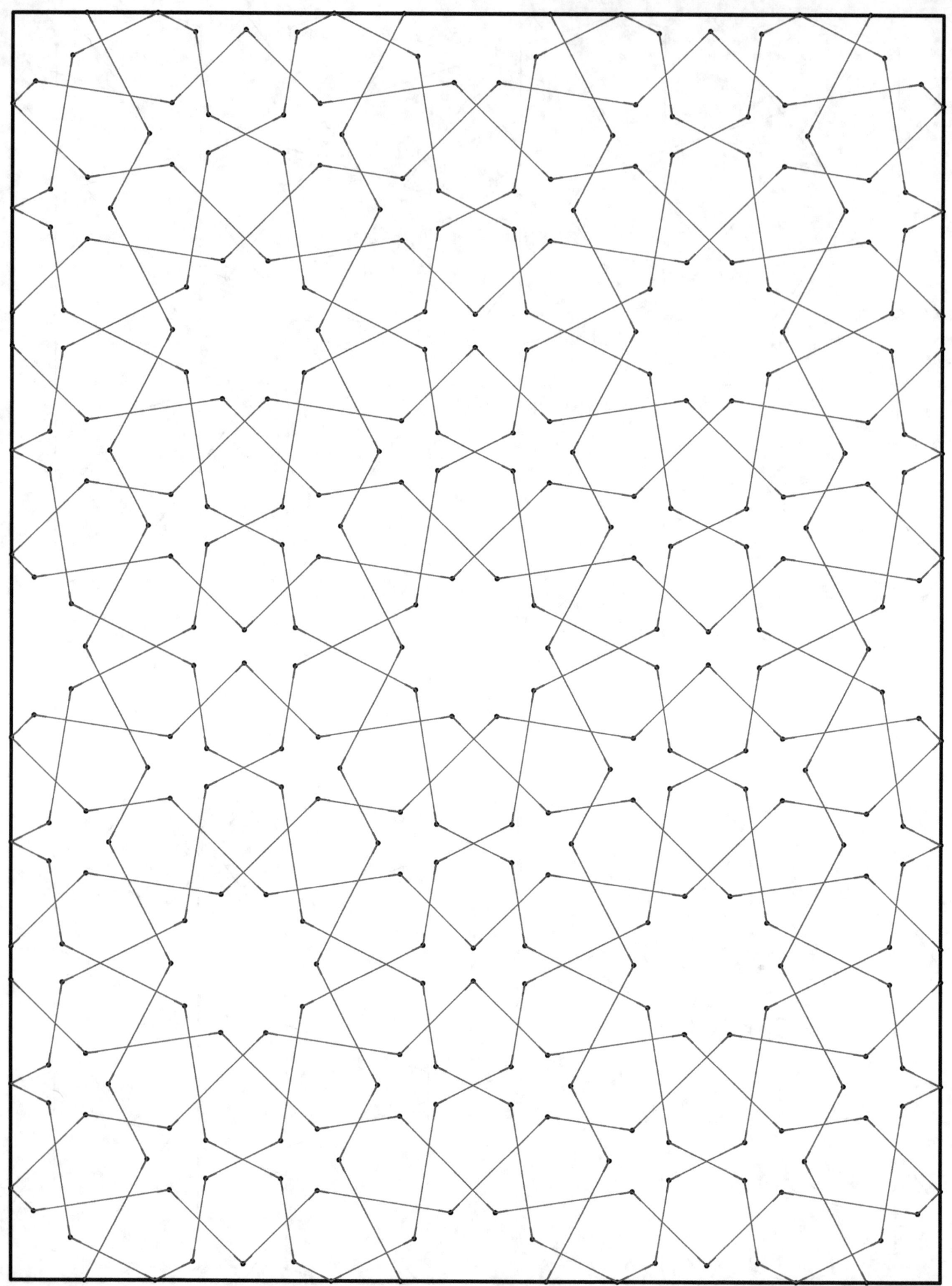

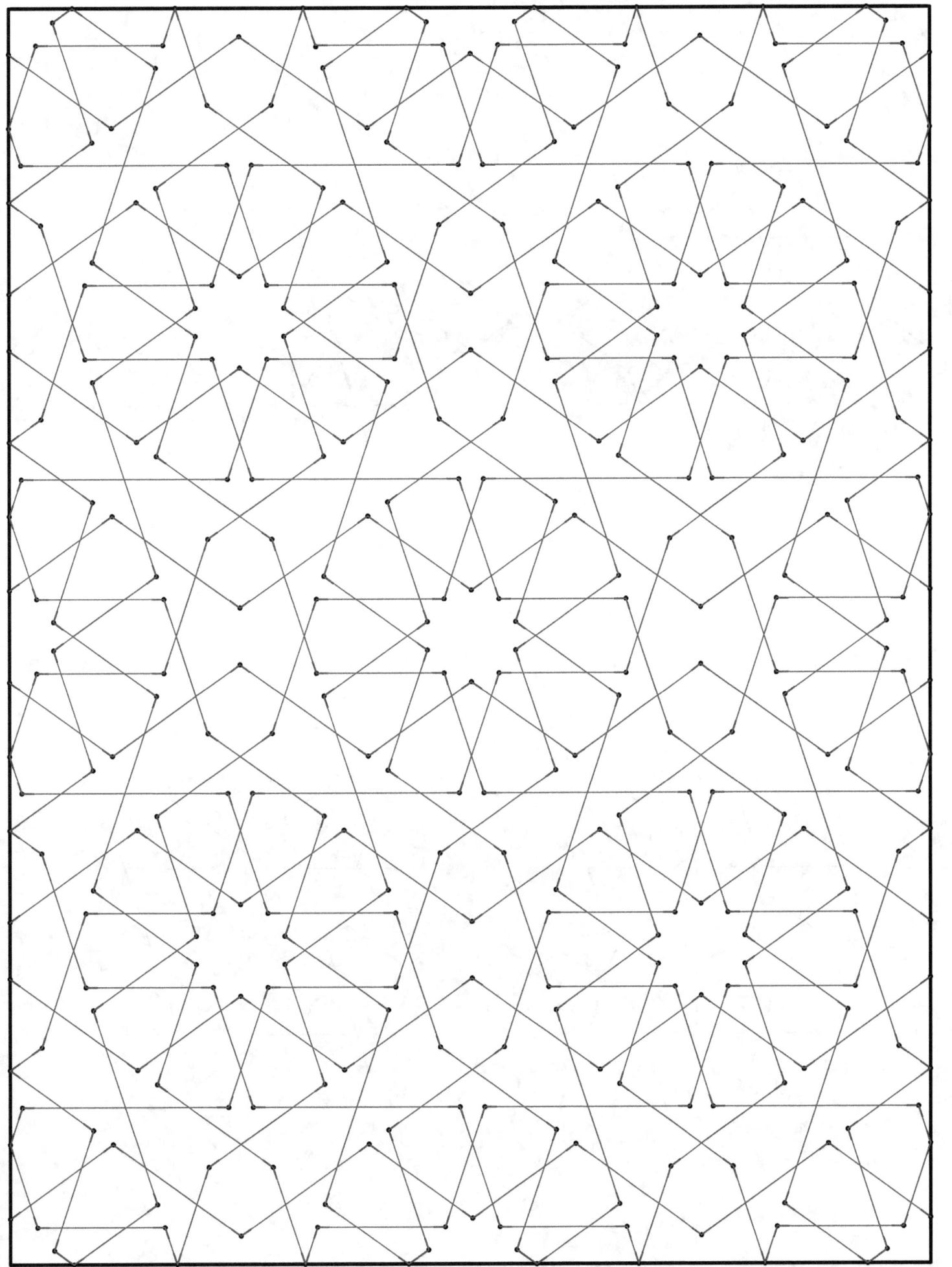

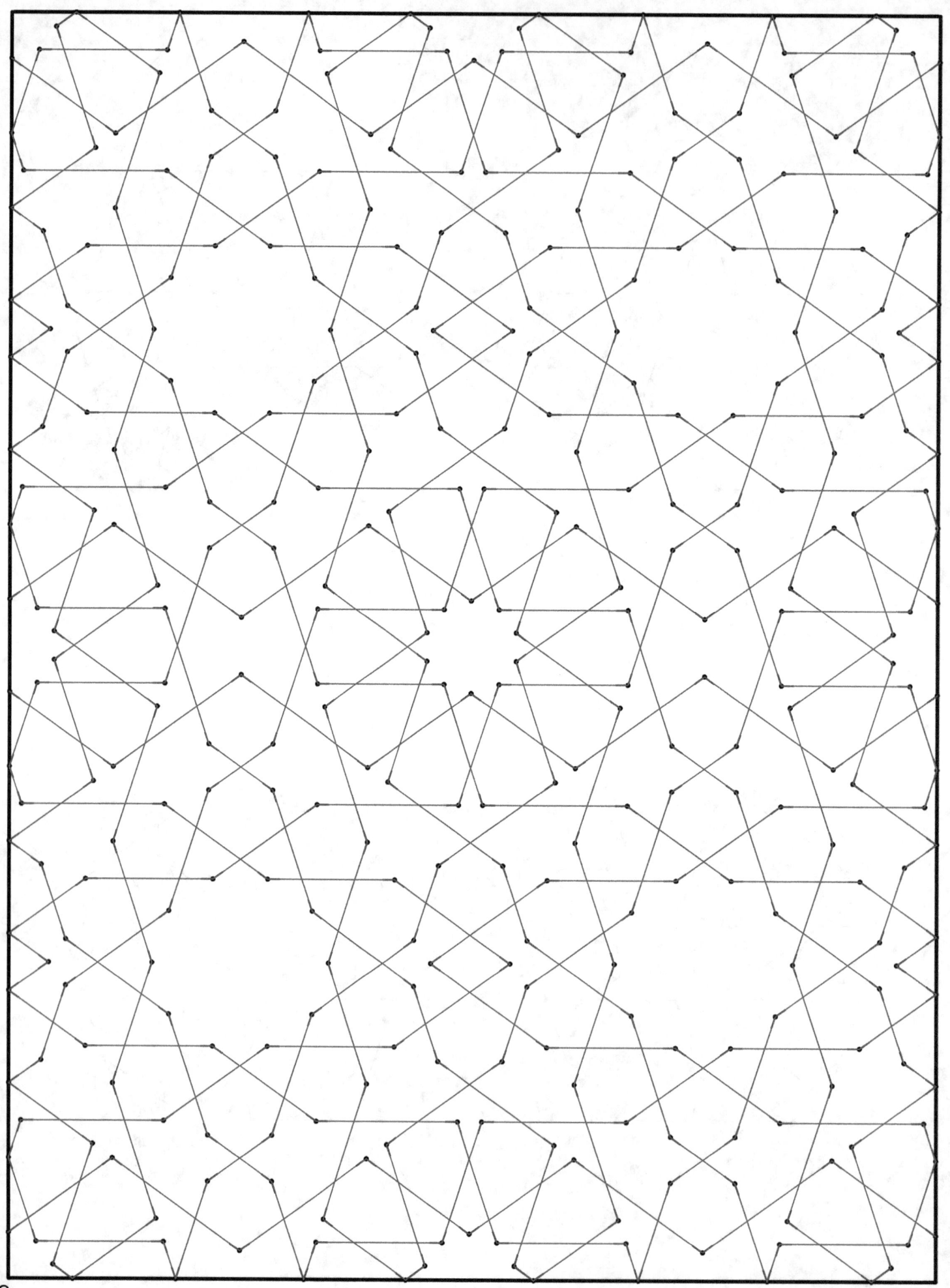

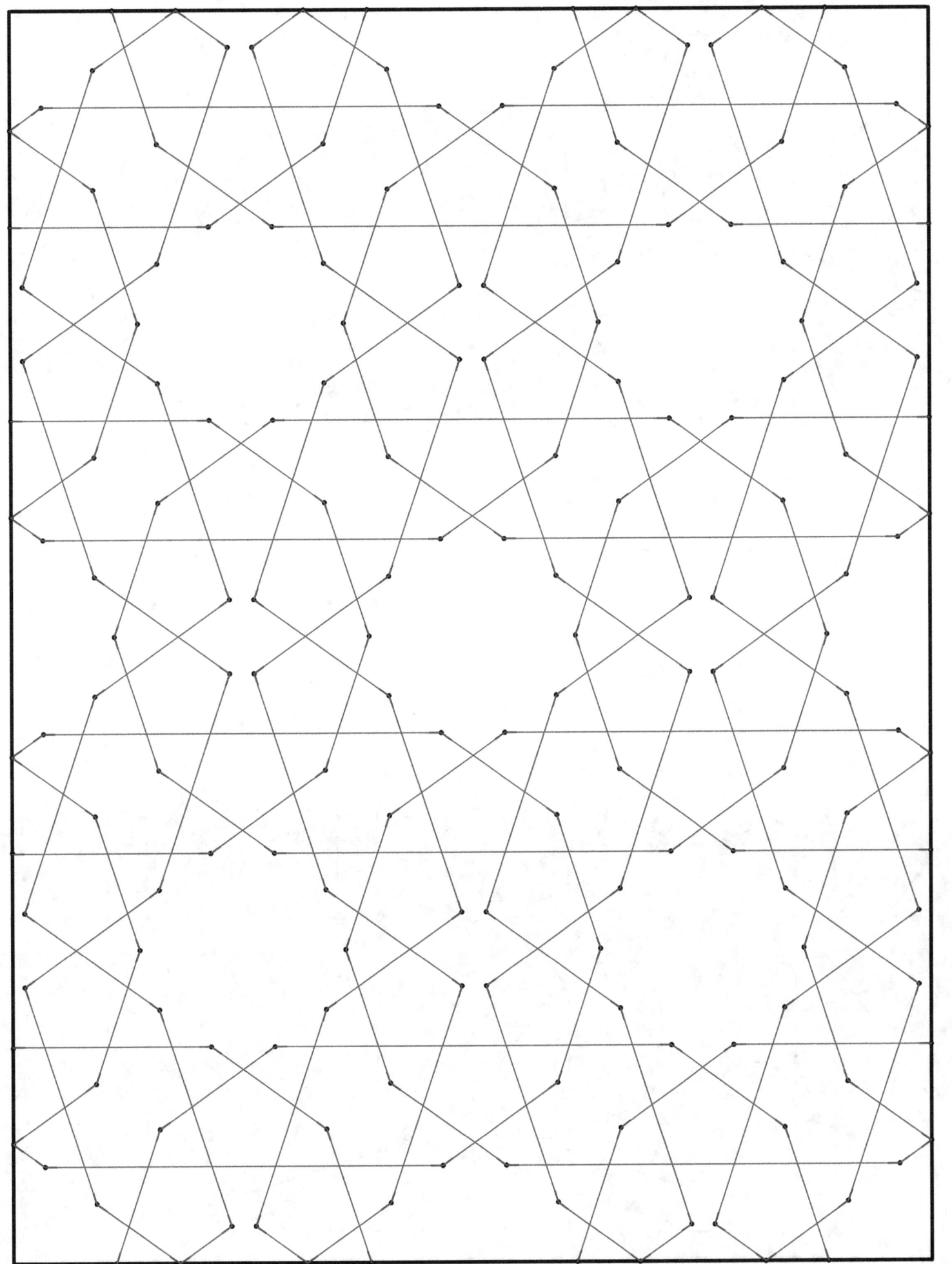

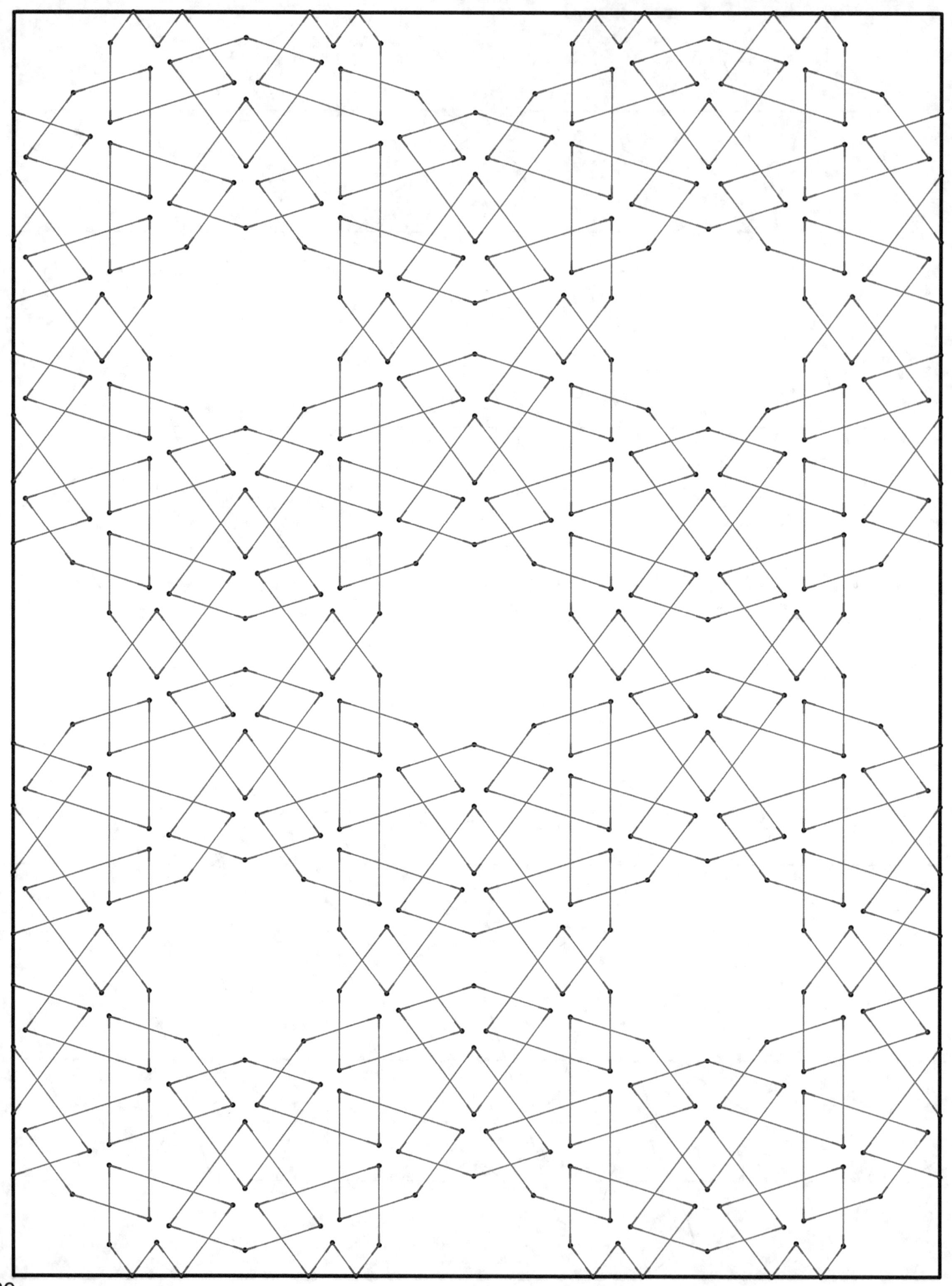

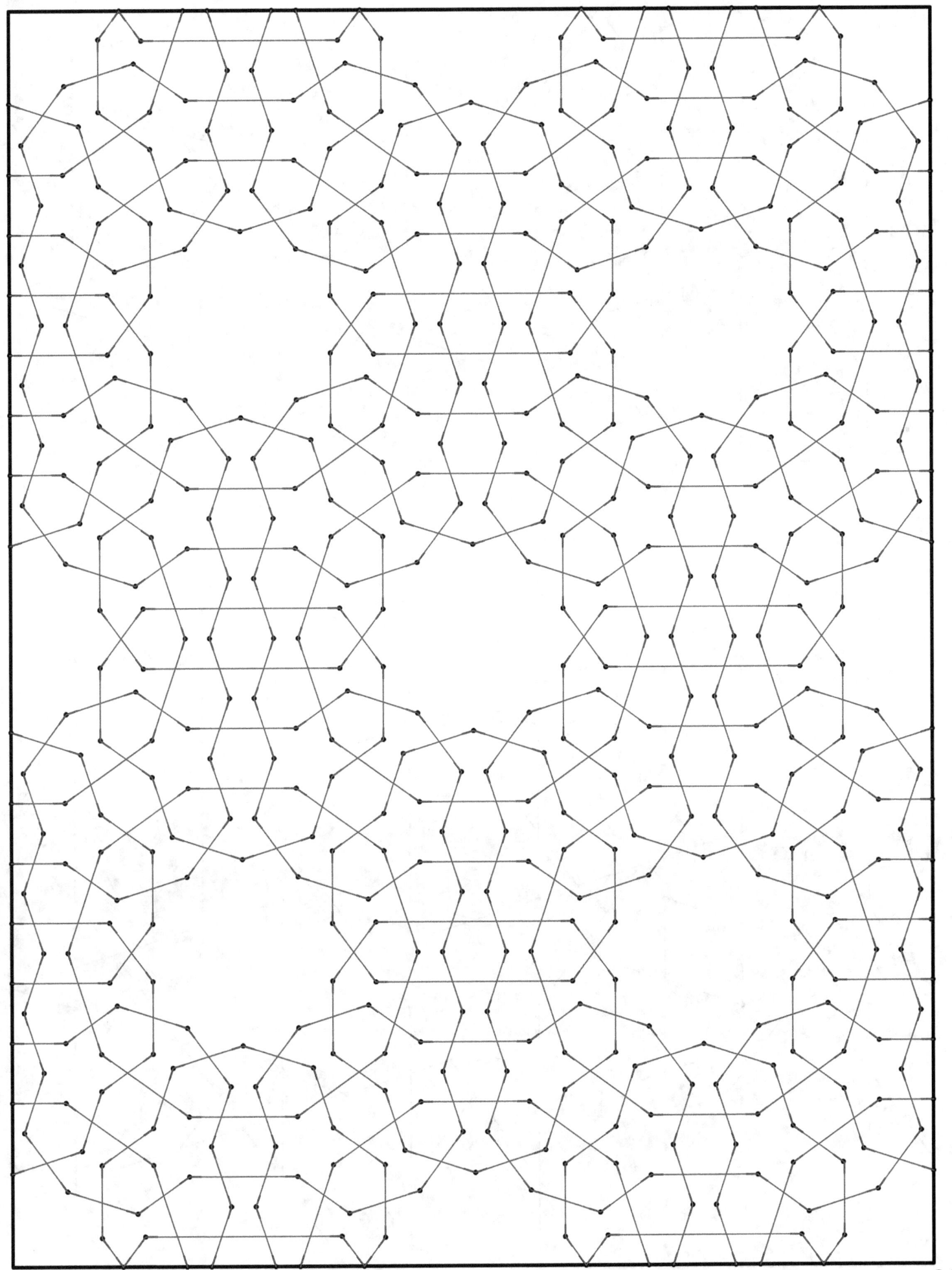

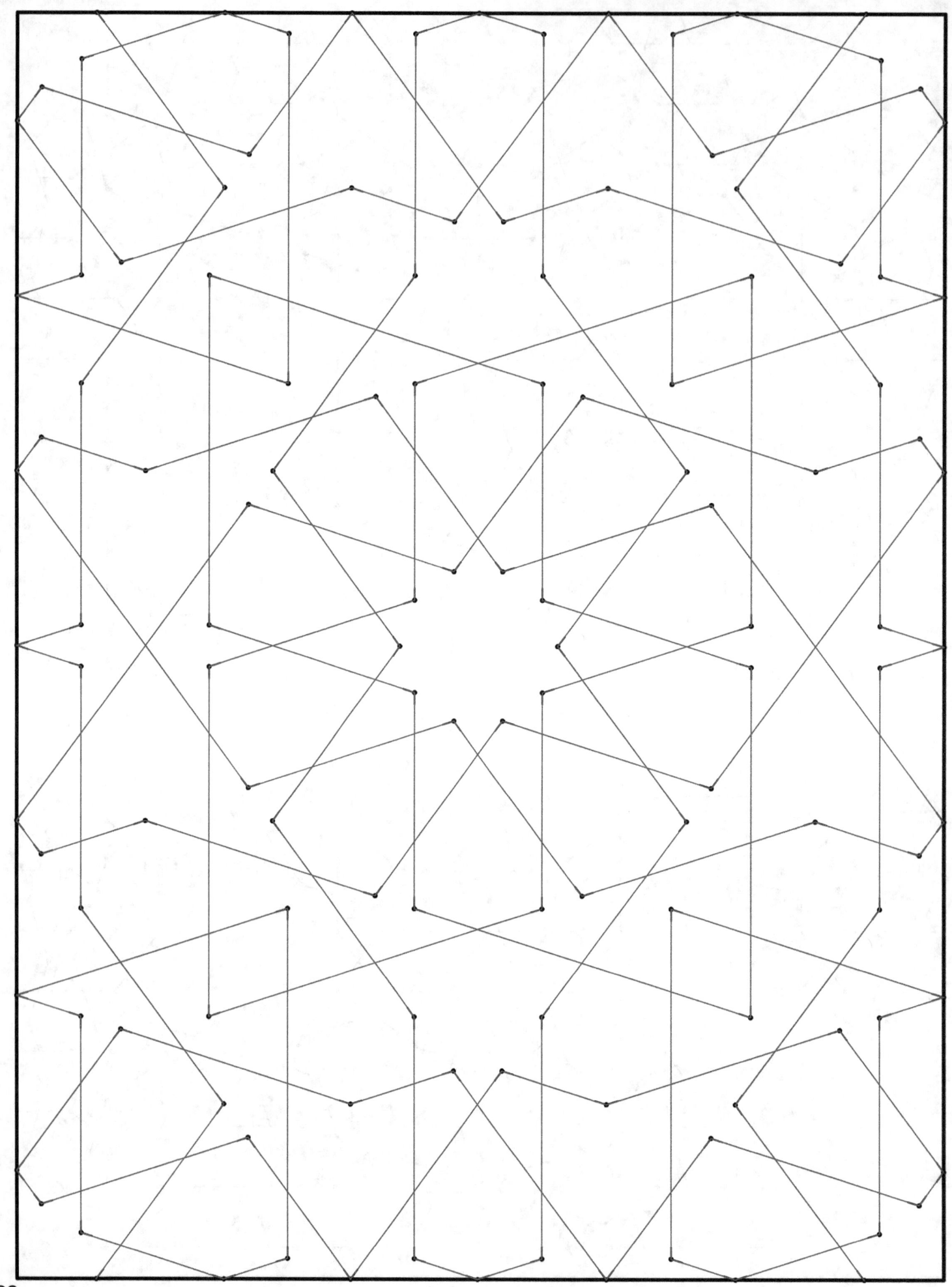

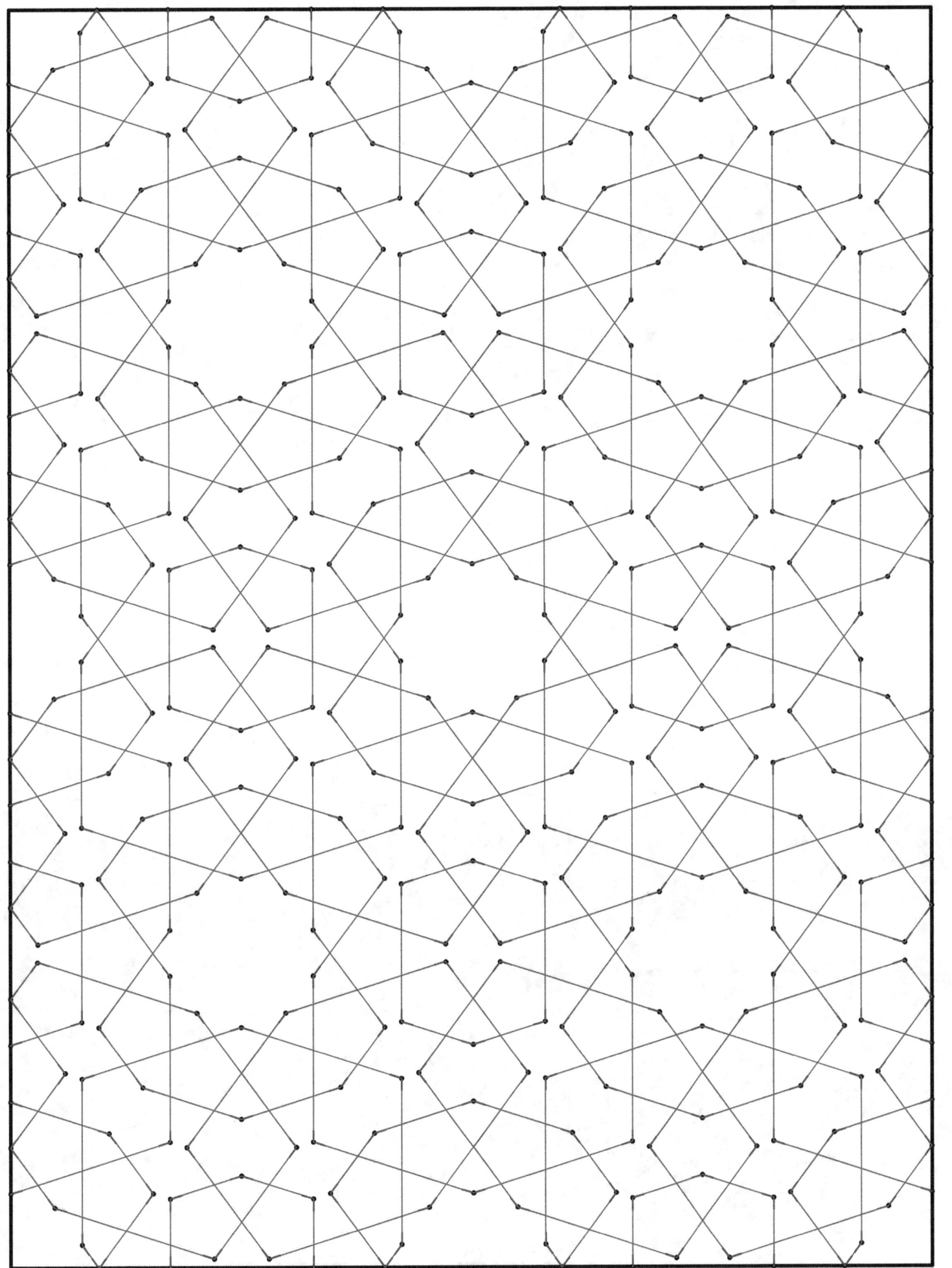

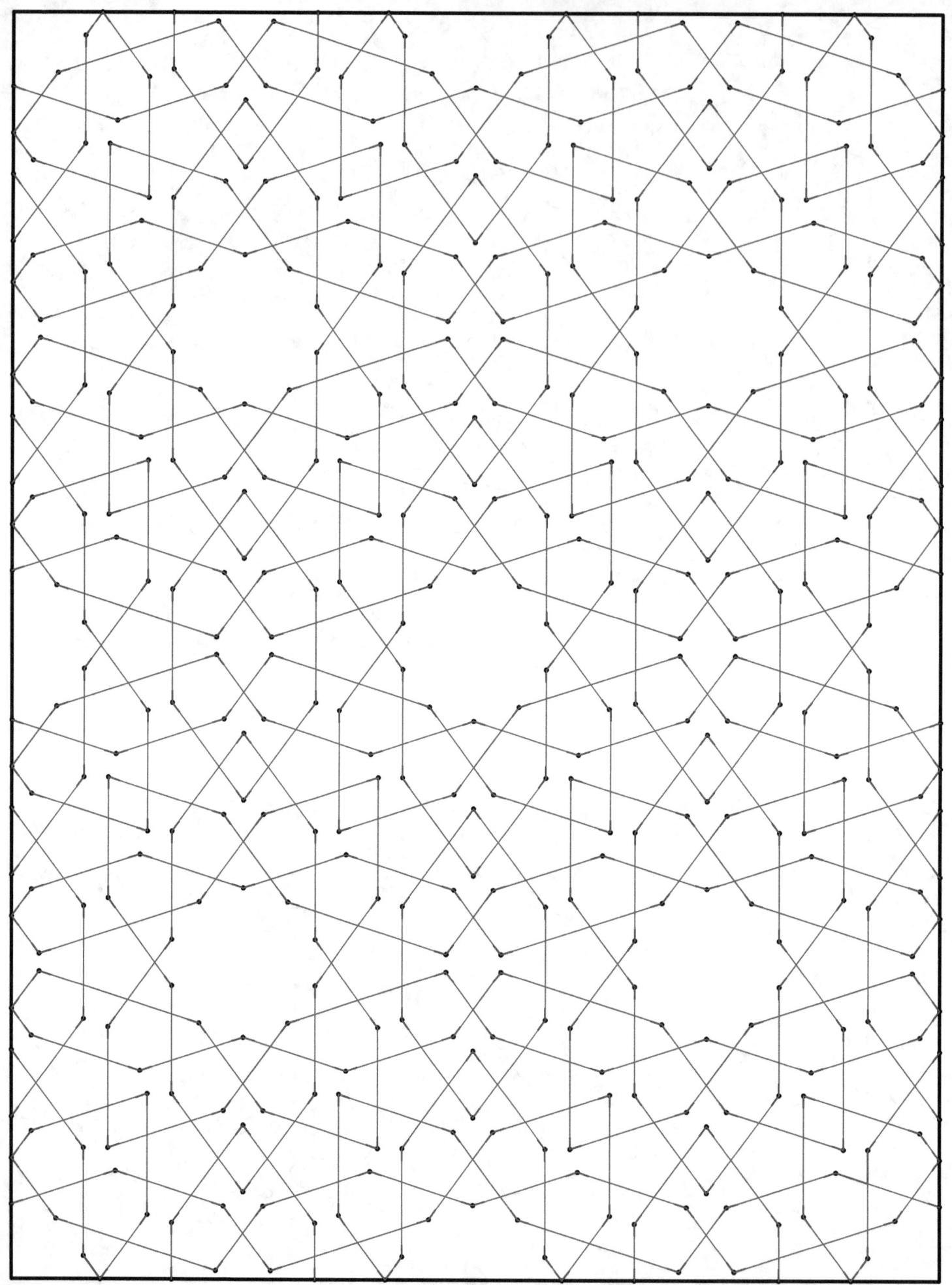

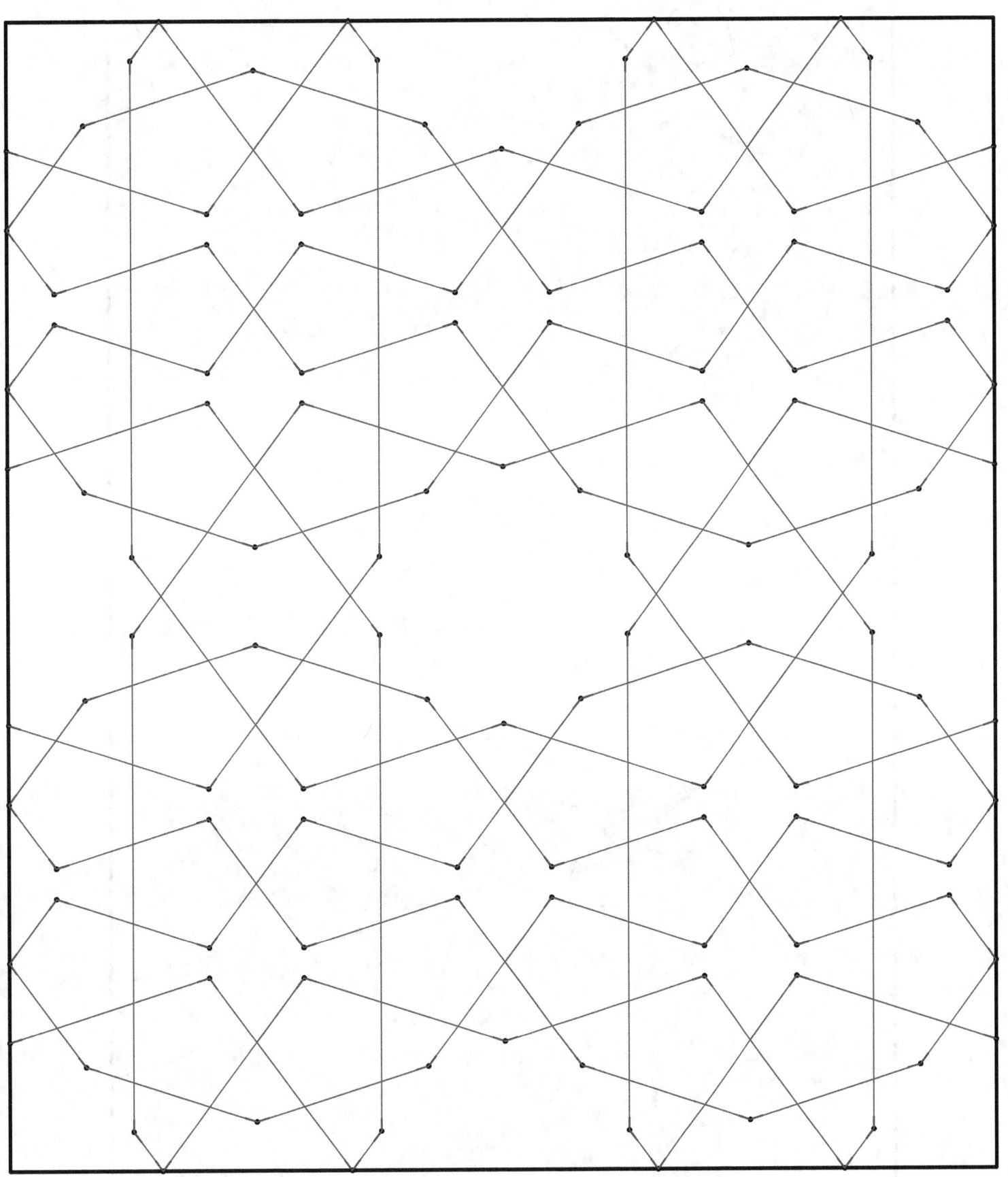

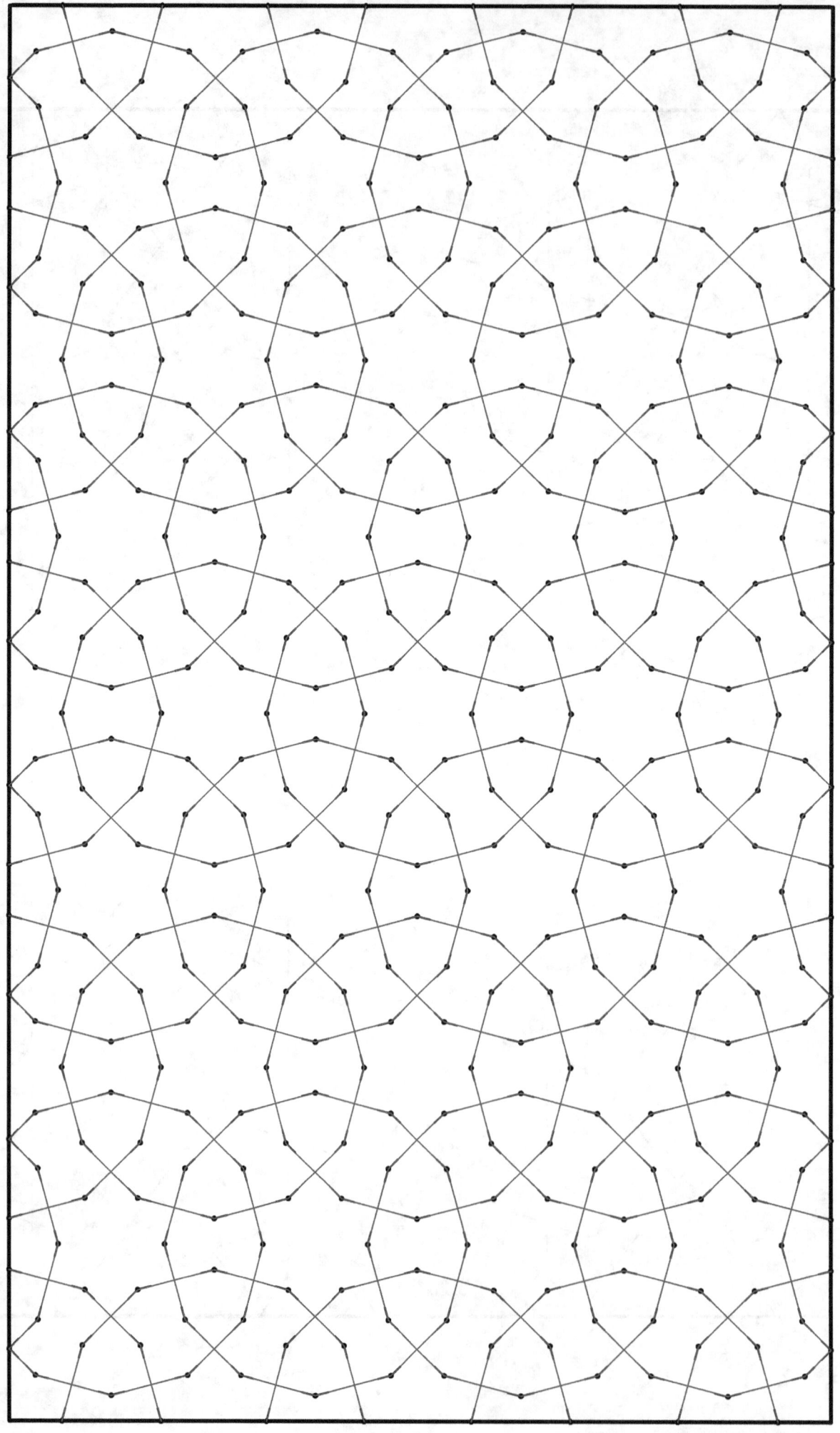

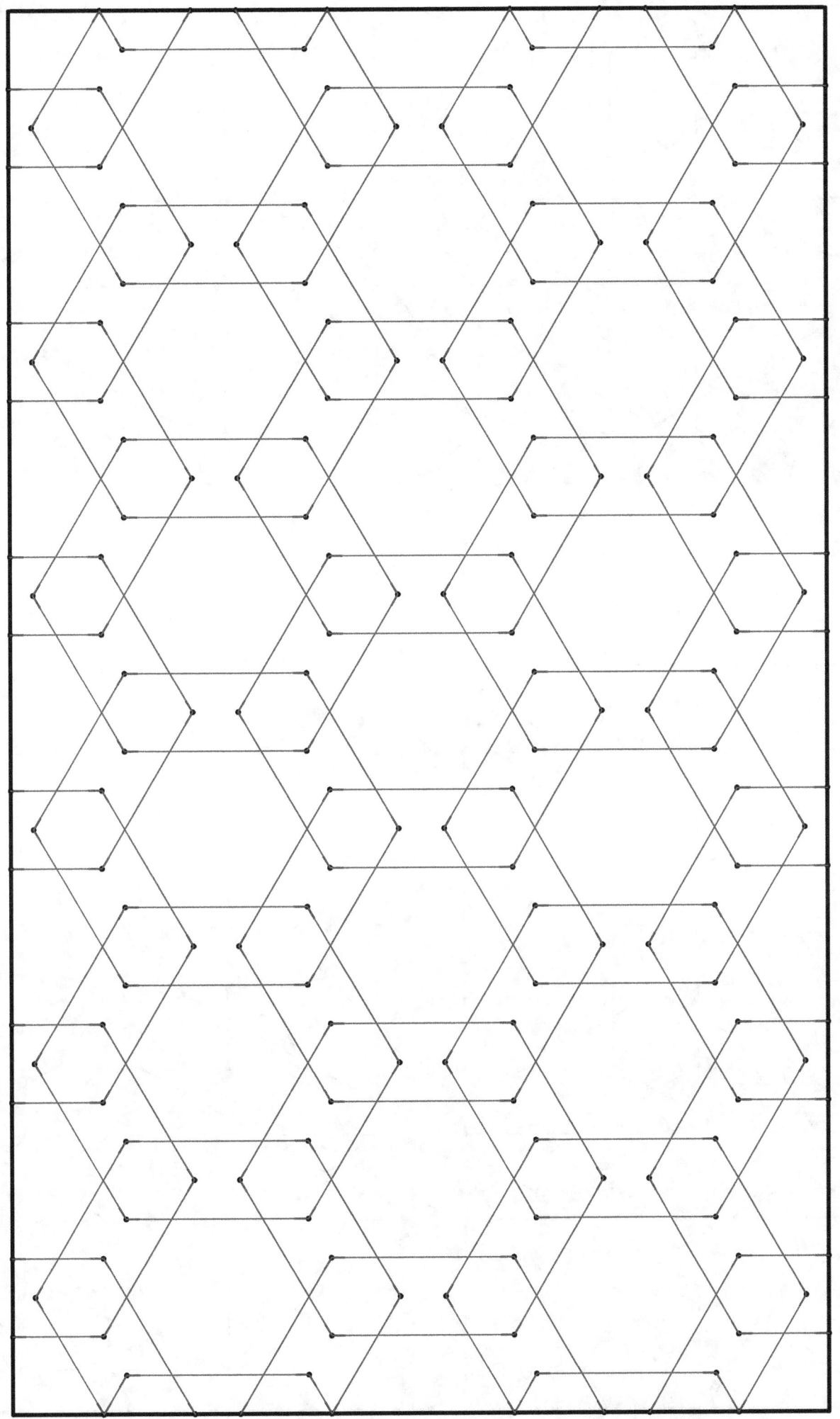

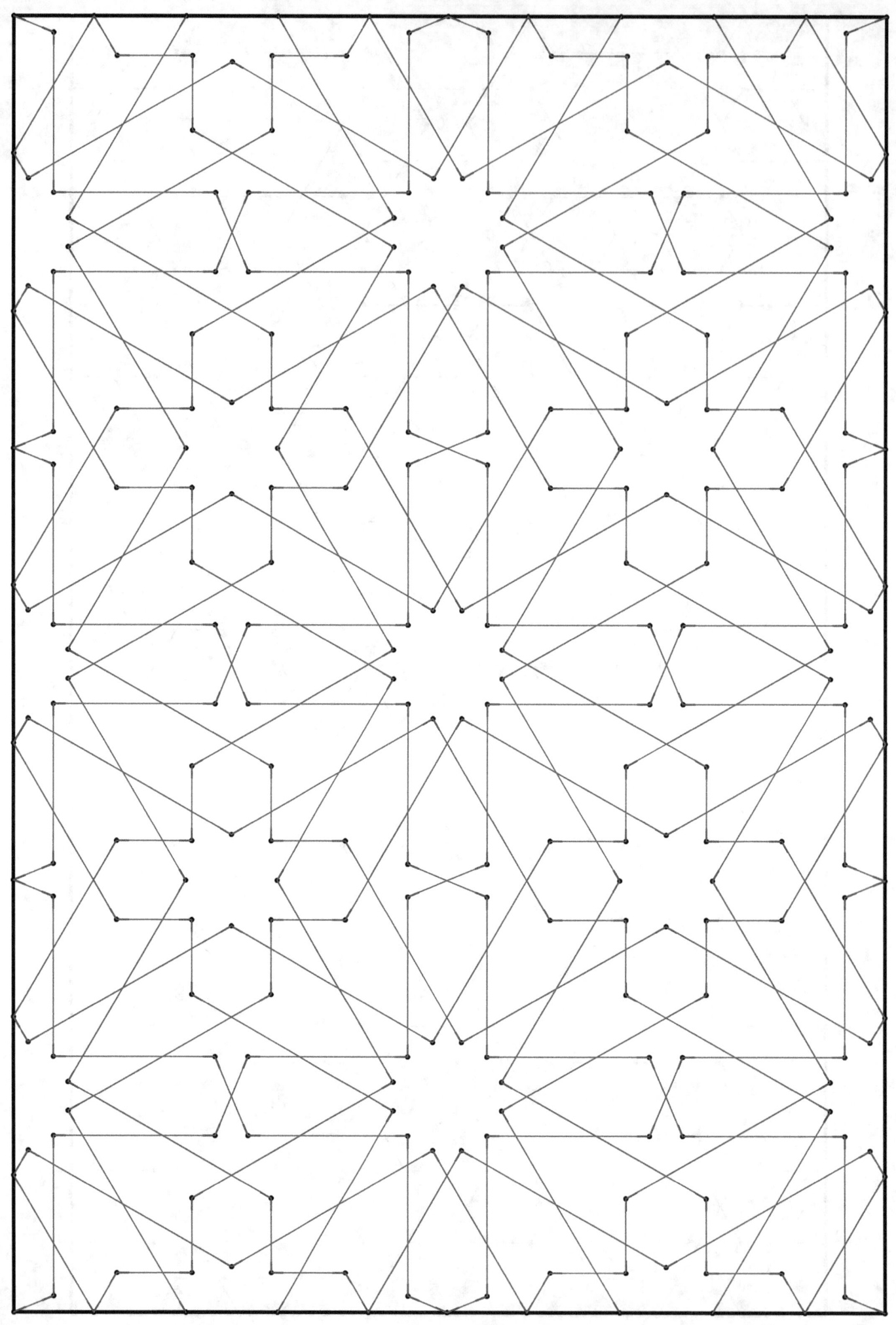

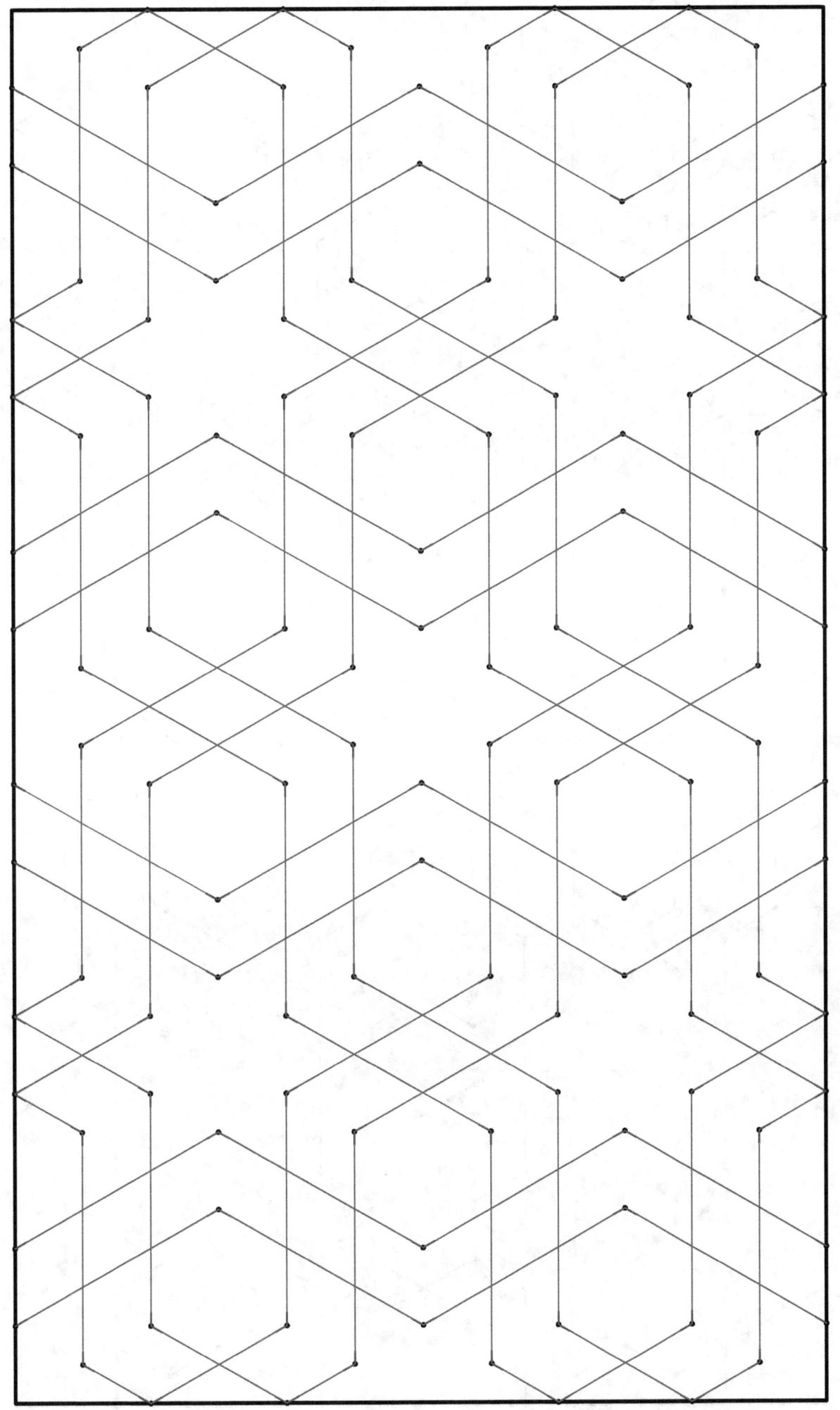

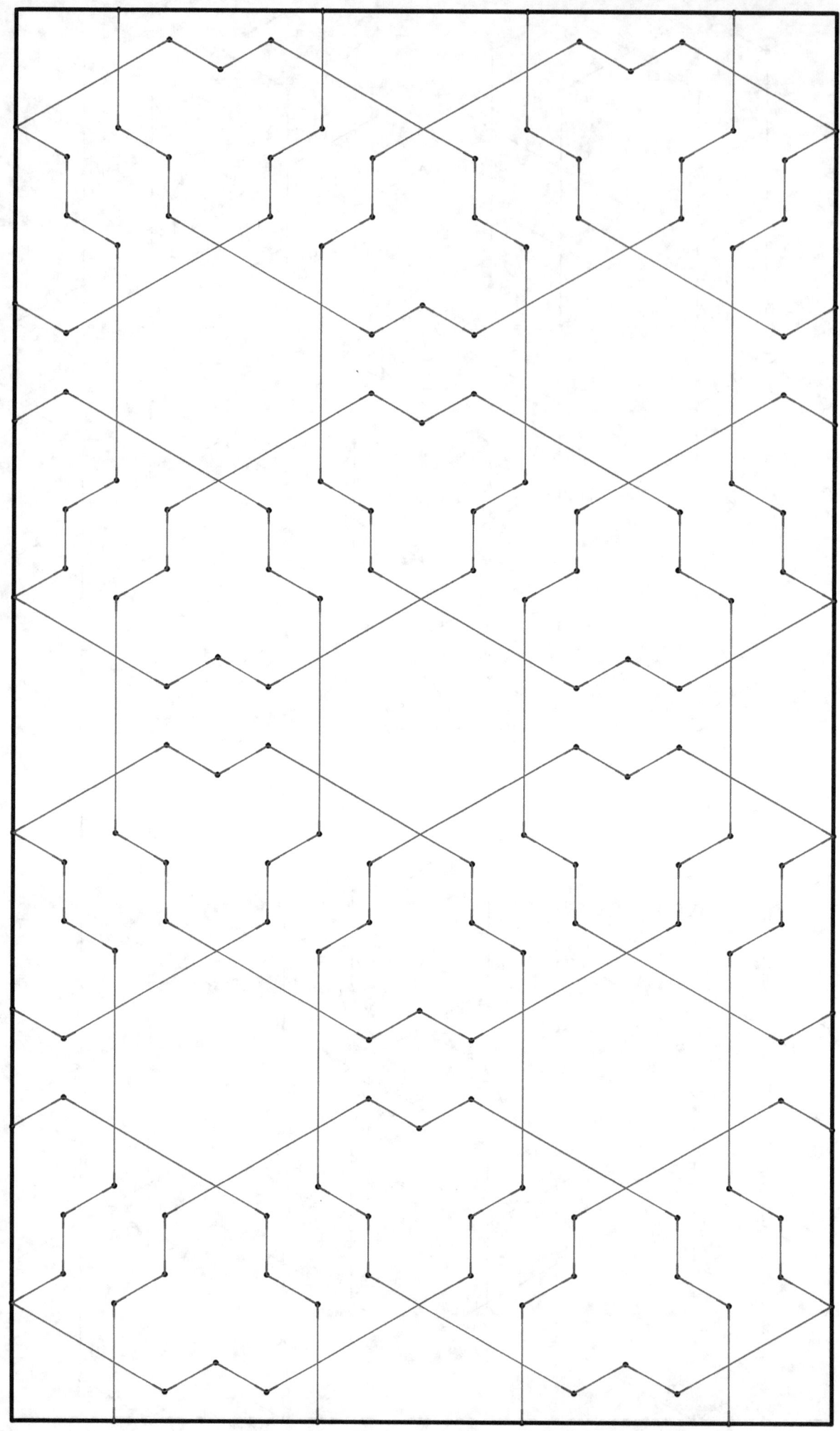

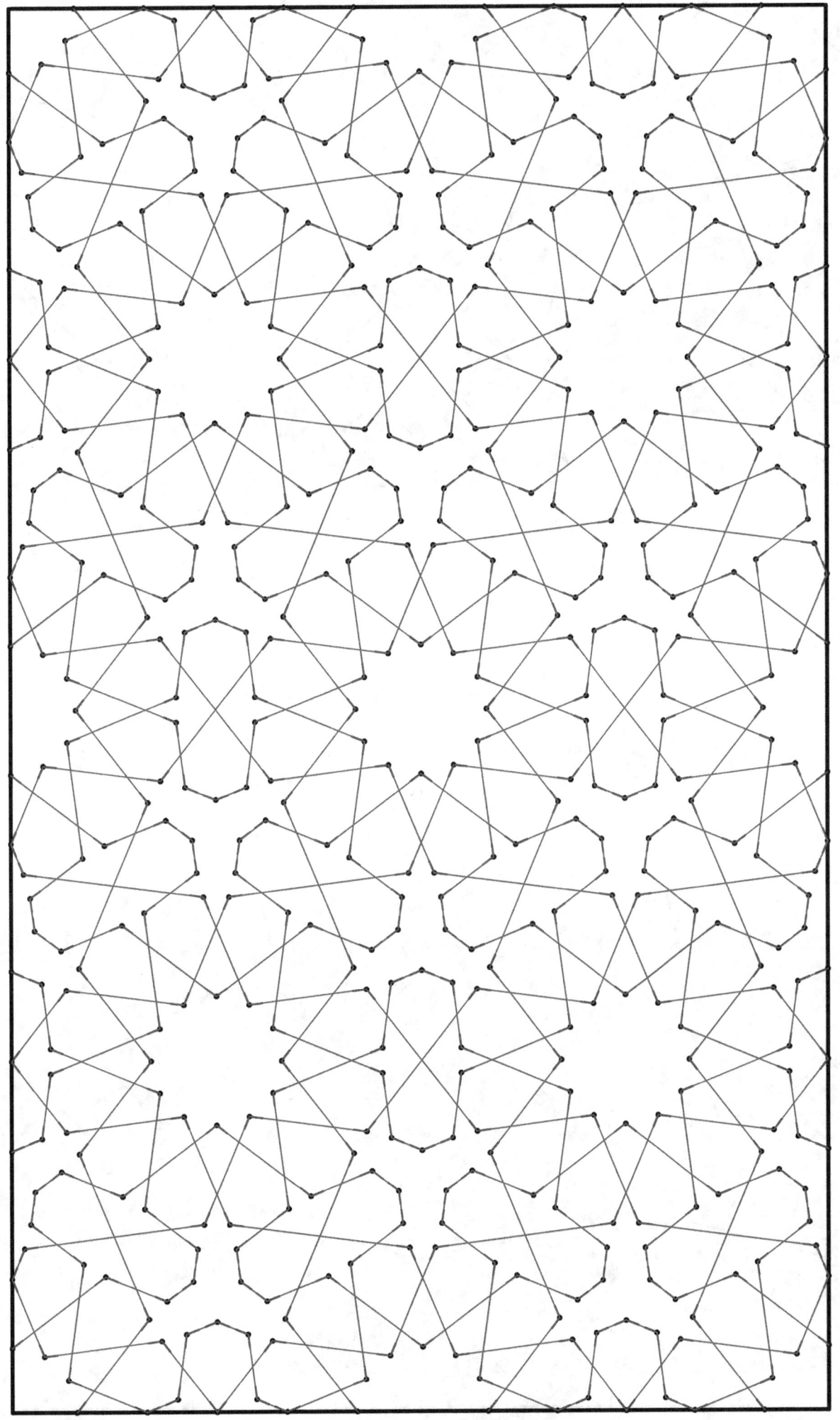

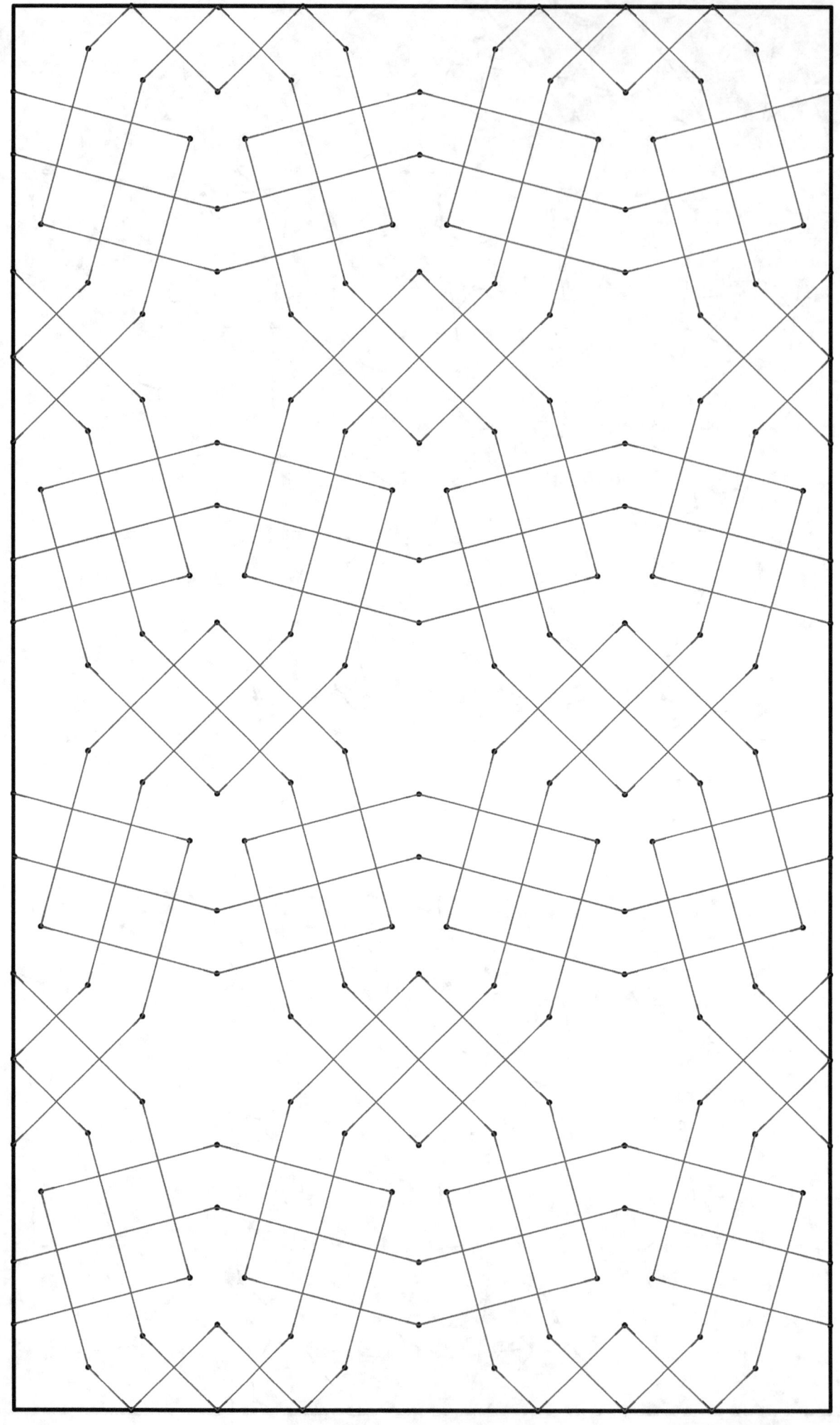

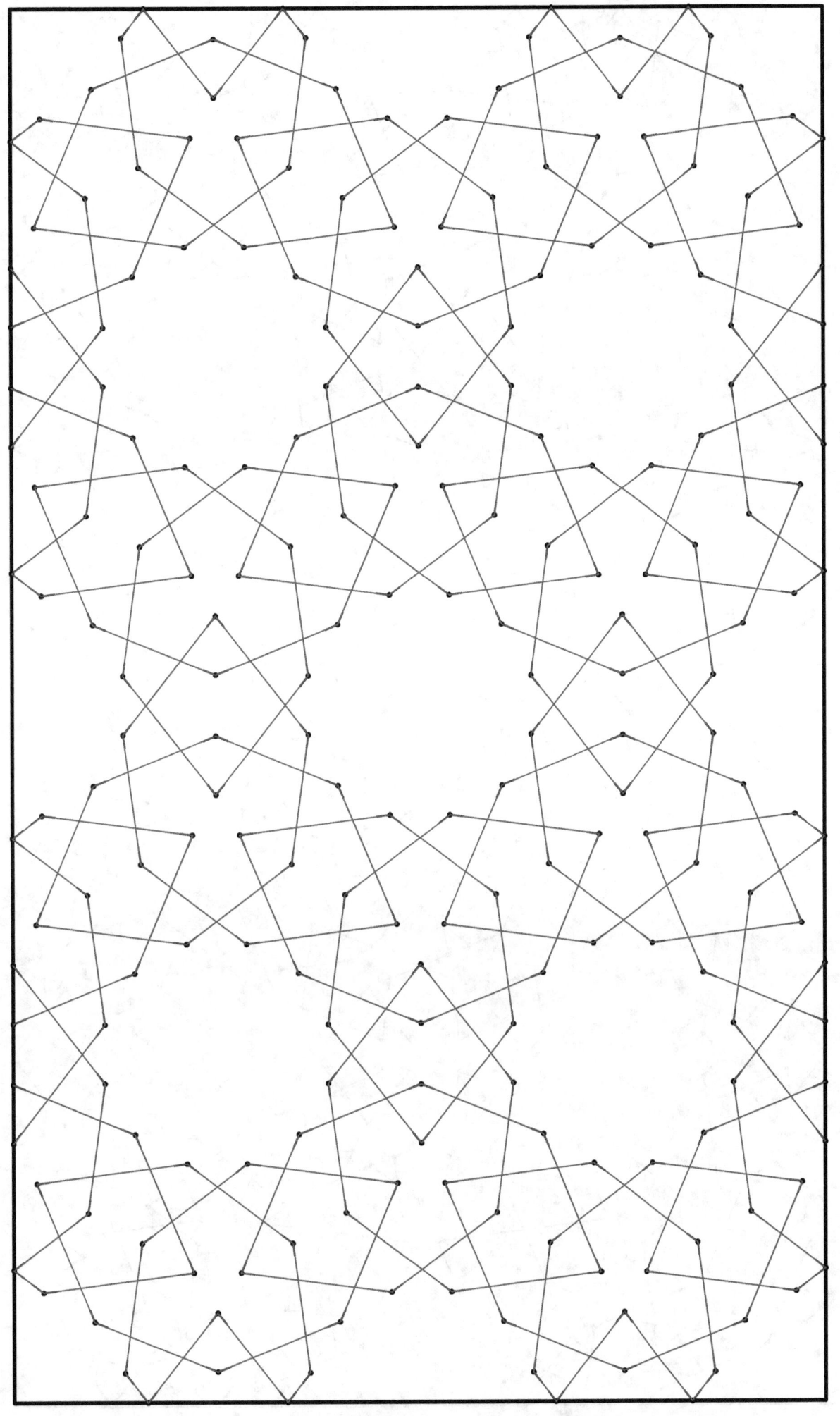

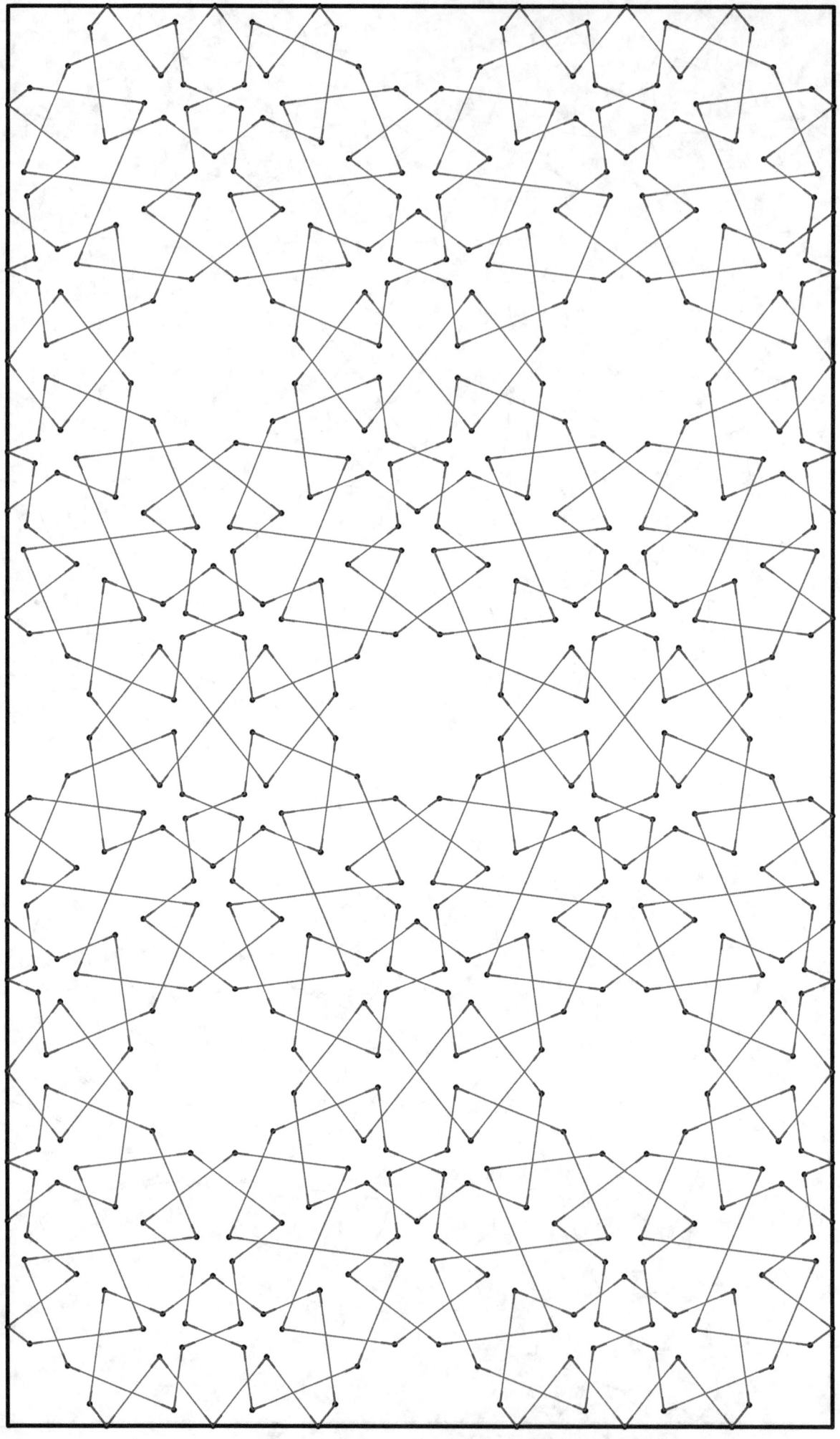

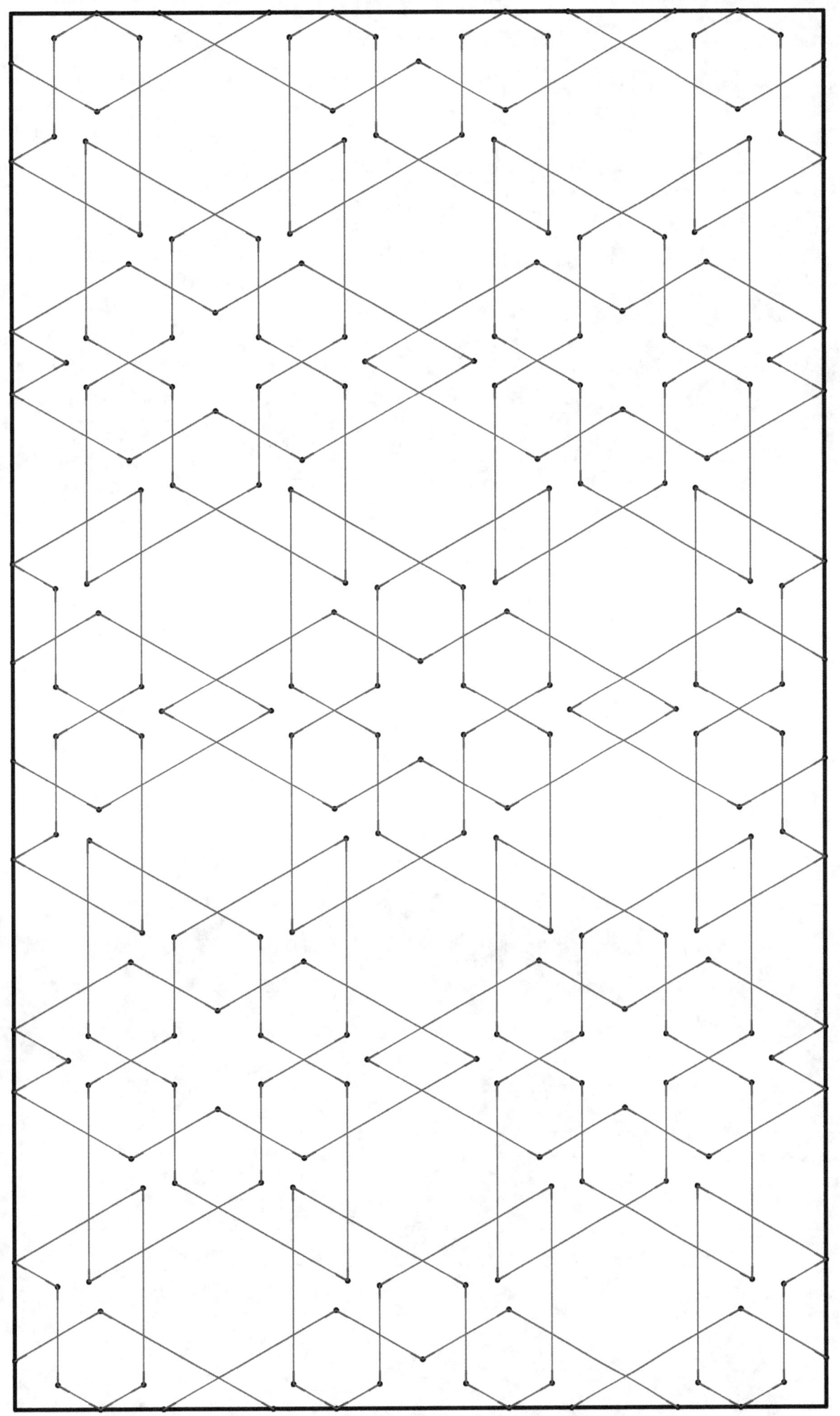

www.ingramcontent.com/pod-product-compliance
Lightning Source LLC
Chambersburg PA
CBHW080513220526

45465CB00006B/2468